Commando

Commando

Brigadier Peter Young DSO MC

PHOTO CREDITS:
Photographs for this book were especially selected from the following Archives: from left to right page 2–3 Imperial War Museum; 7 IWM; 9 IWM; 10 IWM; 11 IWM; 15 IWM; 17 IWM; 18–19 IWM; 20–21 IWM; 20 IWM; 21 The Guards' Magazine IWM; 23 IWM; 25 IWM; 26–27 IWM; 28 IWM; 29 IWM; 30 IWM; 30–31 IWM; 31 IWM; 32–33 IWM; 34 IWM; 35 IWM; 36 Keystone; 37 Radio Times Hulton Picture Library; 39 Keystone; 40 IWM; 41 IWM; 43 Associated Press; 44–45 IWM; 49 IWM; 50 IWM; 53 Sergeant J Terry/IWM; 54–55 Geoffrey Keyes VC of the Rommel Raid by Elizabeth Keyes published by George Newnes; 57 IWM; 59 IWM; 60–61 IWM; 64 IWM; 65 IWM; 66–67 IWM; 66 IWM; 67 IWM; 68 IWM; 68–69 IWM; 71 Brigadier Peter Young; 72–73 IWM; 74–75 IWM; 76 IWM; 77 IWM; 78 IWM; 80–81 IWM; 83 IWM; 84 IWM; 85 IWM; 87 Brigadier Peter Young Keystone; 88–89 Ullstein; 89 Associated Press Ullstein; 90–91 IWM; 93 IWM; 96 IWM; 97 IWM; 99 Colonel SW Chant-Sempill; 101 Sado Opera Mundi; 104–105 IWM; 106–107 'The Greatest Raid of All' by CE Lucas Phillips published by William Heinemann; 108–109 IWM; 110 Suddeutscher Verlag; 111 'The Greatest Raid of All'; 112–113 'The Greatest Raid of All'; 114–115 IWM; 116–117 IWM; 118–119 IWM; 120 IWM; 121 IWM; 123 IWM; 124 'Geoffrey' by JE Appleyard published by The Blandford Press; 125 'Geoffrey'; 130–131 IWM; 132–133 IWM; 134–135 IWM; 138–139 IWM/Ullstein; 140 IWM; 143 IWM; 144 'Commando' by John Durnford-Slater published by William Kimber/Brigadier Peter Young; 146 Ullstein/Sado Opera Mundi; 147 IWM; 148 IWM; 150–151 IWM; 152–153 IWM; 154–155 IWM; 158–159 IWM.

ISBN 0-345-25890-8-250

Manufactured in the United States of America

First Edition: November 1969
Second Printing: April 1977

Editor-in-Chief: Barrie Pitt
Art Director: Peter Dunbar
Military Consultant: Sir Basil Liddell Hart
Picture Editor: Robert Hunt
Executive Editor: David Mason
Art Editor: Sarah Kingham
Designer: John Marsh
Research Assistant: Yvonne Marsh
Cartographer: Richard Natkiel
Special Drawings: John Batchelor

Contents

6   Introduction

8   The beginnings

16   Lofoten and Spitzbergen

38   The adventures of Layforce

56   Vaagso

92   St Nazaire

114   Alarums and excursions

128   Dieppe

156   Epilogue

160   Bibliography

Assault

Brigadier Anthony Farrar-Hockley
DSO MBE MC

The Allied victory in 1945, so successful, so complete, tends to diminish our memories of the early years of the Second World War when, far from seeing a prospect of victory, almost every horizon reflected tidings of continued defeat.

In these years of disaster and loss, what sustained us was a sense of outrage, and hence a determination to recover what had been taken from us – not matter how long it took or how much of our lifeblood was involved.

Such an end could only be attained ultimately by offensive action. In the early summer of 1940, Britain was attempting to organise as best it could, its defeated army and its weak air force to resist the next anticipated phase of Nazi aggression: invasion of the United Kingdom. The stocks of arms and equipment and the numbers of trained men in Britain, were inadequate to meet the needs of home defence together with the rising calls for reinforcement of the Middle East – so no one might seriously suppose that the time was ripe for offensive operations against the occupied coast across the Channel, or against the hostile coastline which stretched up through Denmark to the tip of Norway in the Arctic circle.

Nonetheless, some men were thinking of immediate offensive action even while British troops were still crossing over from Dunkirk. Recognising that attack on the grand scale was out of the question, the Prime Minister and others were ready to accept temporarily a lesser form: raiding.

As ever, a new concept, a new organisation tends to be resisted, even at a peak of crisis in a nation's affairs. Thus the idea of a special raiding organisation, of units specially recruited and organised for this work, tended to be opposed, sometimes deliberately obstructed. Fortunately, the influence of the Prime Minister and the enthusiasm of a sufficient number of soldiers, sailors and airmen, brought into being the Commandos.

Brigadier Peter Young is a founder-member of this select body. What he has written is a short history of their activities from inception to the Dieppe Raid of August 1942. Not surprisingly, it reads like an adventure story; for that is what the Commandos engaged in – a series of grim adventures from which a high number did not return. Their adventures not only raised the alarm along the occupied coast line – they raised the morale of the Allied sympathisers everywhere, progressively, as the scope and the range of their operations spread from Europe to the Mediterranean coastlines.

The units wearing the green beret became legendary. Brigadier Young's narrative tells us why.

6

The beginnings

'Of course, it is absolutely terrific. It is the greatest job in the Army that one could possibly get, and it is a job that, if properly carried out, can be of enormous value . . . no red tape, no paper work . . . just pure operations, the success of which depends principally on oneself and the men one has oneself picked to do the job with you . it's revolutionary.'

The man who invented the Commandos was Lieutenant-Colonel Dudley Clarke. In the grim Dunkirk days he was Military Assistant to the Chief of the Imperial General Staff, General Sir John Dill. Pondering the defeat of the Allies in France and Belgium he wrestled with one of the age old problems of warfare: what does a nation do, when, though its army has been beaten in the field, it does not accept the decision? His mind ranged back to the guerrilla warfare against Napoleon's armies in Spain, and to the Arab Revolt in Palestine, where he himself had served in 1936. 'Could desperate men, armed only with the weapons they could carry, disdaining artillery, baggage trains and all the paraphernalia of supply, carry on guerrilla warfare against an enemy whose forces were stretched out from Narvik to the Pyrenees?' (From *The Green Beret* by H St George Saunders.) This was the problem, and before retiring to bed on 4th June – the last of the nine days of Dunkirk – the colonel sat down in his flat in Stratton Street, Mayfair, and marshalled his ideas 'in note form on a single sheet of writing paper.'

To anyone accustomed to the normal workings of government the next stage of the story is little short of fantastic: 5th June: Clarke tells Dill his idea. 6th June: Dill tells Winston Churchill, the Prime Minister. 8th June: Dill tells Clarke the scheme is approved and that afternoon, Section MO9 of the War Office is brought into being.

Dudley Clarke was ordered to mount a raid across the Channel 'at the earliest possible moment'. The only conditions laid down by the Prime Minister were that no unit should be diverted from its most essential task, the defence of Britain, which might

Lieutenant-Colonel Dudley Clarke

8

Above: General Sir John Dill and Winston S Churchill at a tank demonstration in May 1941. *Right:* The Commando spirit

very soon have to face invasion, and that the guerrillas would have to be content with the minimum quantity of weapons. Both of these conditions were inevitable in the circumstances of the time, and otherwise Clarke was given a free hand.

The Prime Minister's interest and support was a vital factor in imparting a sense of urgency to those concerned with their formation. His thinking is revealed in a minute of 18th June 1940: 'What are the ideas of the C-in-C Home Forces, about 'Storm Troops' or 'Leopards' drawn from existing units, ready to spring at the throat of any small landings or descents? These officers and men should be armed with the latest equipment, tommy guns, grenades, etc., and should be given great facilities in motor-cycles and armoured cars.'

The next problem was to raise a raiding force. This could either be done by taking existing battalions from Home Forces or by raising fresh units. The latter solution was adopted, a decision which for various reasons was a wise one. Commanding officers and a number of the company commanders were in their forties, decidedly on the old side for raiding. The ranks of units belonging to Home Forces were full of reservists and young conscripts, some too cautious and others too inexperienced to guarantee results in operations where 'the book' – Field Service Regulations – would provide no guidance, and where the deadly and the impossible would be normal. Moreover, the war establishment (or organization) of a standard infantry battalion, designed to take its place in a prolonged campaign, was not necessarily the most suitable for a light raiding force. Considerations of this sort led to the decision to form a new style unit, the Commando. Its name was taken from mobile Boer units, which for some two years had defied 250,000 British troops during the Boer War (1899–1902). The original organization, a headquarters and ten troops each of three officers and forty-seven other

ranks, owed nothing to the establishment of a battalion. If anything it harked back to the 18th Century rangers and light corps which made their names under men like Rogers, Marion 'the Swamp Fox', Ewald, and Tarleton.

The cadre of Numbers 1 and 2 Commandos came from the ten Independent Companies raised earlier in the year when the Germans invaded Norway. They were composed for the most part of volunteers from the Territorial Army, and were intended to raid the enemy lines of communication. As things turned out they had done no raiding though about half of them had seen action fighting desperate rearguard actions in the snowclad valleys around Bodo and Mo.

The other commandos were formed by calling for volunteers for special service. Commanding officers were selected from among the volunteers. They were then given a free hand to choose their own officers. Thereafter the three officers of each troop drove round the various units allotted to them and recruited their own men.

This rough and ready system worked pretty well. The original commanding officers included Bob Laycock from the Royal Horse Guards; John Durnford-Slater from the Royal Artillery; and Ronnie Tod from the Argyll and Sutherland Highlanders. Before the war was ended the first of these was to become a major-general and Chief of Combined Operations, while the last two became brigadiers.

The letter which outlined the conditions of this special service was not particularly revealing. One officer who joined at the outset recalls that: 'Commanding Officers were to ensure that only the best were sent; they must be young, absolutely fit, able to drive motor vehicles, and unable to be seasick. It was a leap in the dark, for absolutely nothing was said as to what they were to do, and in any case most regular officers make a point of never volunteering for anything.' Be that as it may, no less than ten of the original officers of Number 3 Commando were regulars. One of the conditions of service, clearly laid down, was that any man might voluntarily return to his unit, after an operation. Few ever asked to do so.

Indeed to be RTU (returned to unit) was the fate most dreaded by Commando soldiers.

Something like one hundred troops were formed and practically every regiment and corps of the British Army must have been represented. Regulars, reservists and territorials from every part of the country were to be found in their ranks and one can hardly say that any troop was typical. H Troop of Number 3 Commando, in which the present writer served, was selected from men of the 4th Division, which had fought with some tenacity in the Dunkirk campaign. The men, though they included soldiers from the Royal Artillery, the Royal Engineers and the Royal Army Service Corps, were for the most part selected from the county regiments, the backbone of the British Infantry. For the most part they were reservists, but there was a leavening of regulars. The majority had served in India, and were skilled men-at-arms. They had been in action and wanted more. This troop was perhaps exceptional, but all were determined to excel. Before June was out this Commando had assembled at Plymouth, and all over the country the new units were springing to life.

Not the least remarkable of the many strange things about the history of the Commandos is that their first raid took place only nineteen days after their formation. It cannot be claimed that it was an epoch-making event, but at least it was a step on the long road back to Europe, the road to victory.

The planning of military operations is never precisely easy, even without the added complication of a sea crossing. The planning of raids in the summer of 1940 presented well-nigh every obstacle that the most pessimistic planner's nightmares could conjure up. But the men who conceived the Commandos were optimists. In the summer when Winston Churchill was inspiring his countrymen with promises of blood, sweat, toil and tears, pessimism, however well founded, was not in season. It was just as well. To plan a raid one needs a wide choice of suitable targets, and accurate information as to enemy forces and their deployment in the area of the objective. Up to June 1940 all the resources of British Intelligence had been concentrated on the German build-up on the Western Front. Now the coast of Europe from Narvik to Bayonne had suddenly become the enemy line and the slow piecing together of information, from the reports of agents and from air photography, had to begin all over again.

When Dudley Clarke first went to seek the co-operation of the Admiralty he was cordially received by the Assistant Chief of the Naval Staff: 'What! The Army wants to get back to fight again already? That's the best news I've had for days. For that you can have anything you like to ask for from the Navy.' Captain G A Garnons-Williams was given the task of collecting craft and set up his headquarters in the yacht *Melisande* lying in the Hamble. Motor boats and pleasure craft of every description, and widely differing reliability, were assembled from the Norfolk Broads and anywhere else where in peacetime people had enjoyed themselves 'messing about in boats'.

Willing though the Navy was, combined operations demanded landing-craft, and the very few Britain had possessed in 1939 had been lost in Norway. Still, a service that had so recently improvised a flotilla to bring 338,226 British and French troops from Dunkirk was not unduly troubled by the problem of taking a few hundred men in the other direction. If they had to land from un-armoured craft designed for entirely different purposes, the soldiers did not care – if only because they didn't know any better.

The naval side of planning an operation is complicated by problems of navigation, wind and tide. There are often no more than a few days in any month when a particular beach or landing place will be practicable. When so many things can go wrong it is just as well to load the dice as much as possible. This in itself is sufficient justification for seeing to it that the troops employed are all picked volunteers.

The first commando raid was carried out on the night of 23rd/24th June, when landings were made in the Boulogne-Le Touquet area. Major Tod was in command of the force, 120 strong, which bore the title of Number 11 Independent Company. Garnons-Williams had managed to borrow half a dozen RAF rescue craft from the Air Ministry. Though fast, reliable, and seaworthy, their bows were high out of the water and therefore they were not ideal for landing craft.

The expedition, whose armament included half of the forty Tommy guns then in the country, sailed from Dover, Folkestone and Newhaven. In mid-Channel Spitfires swooped down to examine them, but fortunately realizing they they were not German patrol boats, refrained from shooting them up. However, this incident caused some delay.

The air-sea rescue craft lacked sophisticated navigational devices, and Tod was on the point of entering Boulogne harbour when an enemy searchlight suddenly revealed the position. They made off down the coast and landed in some sand dunes, where they had an indecisive brush with a German patrol. The only casualty was Dudley Clarke, who had accompanied the expedition as an observer. A bullet struck him a glancing blow and nearly severed an ear. Thus it chanced that the man who conjured up the idea of the Commandos was the first of them to be wounded.

Another party landed at the Plage de Merlimont, four miles south of Le Touquet, and attacked a large building surrounded by a deep belt of barbed wire. They killed the two sentries and then, unable to make their way through the wire, threw Mills grenades through the windows. Whether the building was a billet, an officers' mess or a headquarters cannot be said, but one may assume that the inmates were not pleased.

At Dover the returning craft were cheered by every ship in the harbour, at Folkestone the arrival of thirty dishevelled soldiers was regarded with the utmost suspicion. In the country in general the bald announcement that, less than a month after Dunkirk, the British had, as it were, stuck a pin into Hitler, was well received.

MO9 lost no time in thinking up another thrust. On the night of the 14th/15th July a raid was mounted against the German garrison of Guern-

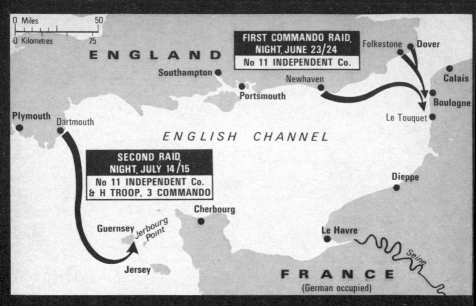

The first Commando raids, which took place in the summer of 1940. The first was launched soon after the formation of the Commandos and resulted in only a skirmish with the occupation forces, but the second, on Guernsey, was a failure, though lessons were learnt in both raids.

HMS Scimitar

sey. This time the intelligence provided was rather impressive. The Germans had been flown in on 1st July, and were 469 strong under a Doktor Maas – their ration strength had been revealed to one of our agents by the contractor.

The force included Major Tod's 11 Independent Company which was to attack the airport, and H Troop, Number 3 Commando, which was to make a feint attack against a machine-gun position at Telegraph Bay and the barracks on the Jerbourg peninsula.

The force was carried in two rather ancient destroyers, *Scimitar* and *Saladin* (1918 vintage) and the landing craft were seven RAF rescue craft. The planning by the newly organized Directorate of Raiding Operations was impressive. It was arranged that Ansons should fly over the island to drown the noise of the landing-craft as they ran in.

The raid was mounted from the Gymnasium of the Naval College, Dartmouth, and some of the cadets helped to load the Tommy gun magazines. An officer who took part in the raid writes: 'After tea in the college dining room we boarded HMS *Scimitar*. Only five of the rescue craft had turned up. We proceeded to sea, increased speed to eighteen knots, and shaped a course for Guernsey. About midnight the rescue craft, which had been keeping station about one hundred

yards away, came alongside and the soldiers transferred to them as silently as possible. The rescue craft made a terrible noise and the sound of the Ansons flying low over Jerbourg peninsula to drown our noise was most welcome. These craft were very high out of the water; moreover, we were very crowded. The idea of coming under aimed small-arms fire in such a craft was unattractive, but no machine gun opened up.'

In fact the Guernsey raid was singularly bloodless, and in general unimpressive. 'Let there be no more Guernseys' said Churchill when he heard of its outcome. It was not quite as simple as that. The Navy, despite inadequate landing craft, played its part with the efficiency and sang-froid that one normally attributes to that unparalleled service. The soldiers lacked an enemy to shoot at, but otherwise played their part. In war lessons are learned and re-learned in odd ways. The survivors of Guernsey went on to greater things.

It was unfortunate that for lack of targets and proper landing craft a false impression of the potential of raiding should so soon have reached the mind of the Prime Minister, the Commandos' greatest supporter.

Two days later Admiral of the Fleet Sir Roger Keyes became Director of Combined Operations. The 68-year-old hero of Gallipoli and Zeebrugge was not the man to break windows with guineas.

Lofoten and Spitzbergen

'After fifteen months experience as Director of Combined Operations, and having been frustrated in every worthwhile offensive action I have tried to undertake, I must fully endorse the Prime Minister's comments on the strength of the negative power which controls the war machine in Whitehall . . . Great leaders of the past have always emphasized the value of time in war . . . time is passing and so long as procrastination, the thief of time, is the key-word of the war machine in Whitehall, we shall continue to lose one opportunity after another during the lifetime of opportunities.'

In October 1941 Sir Roger Keyes, who had seldom seen eye to eye with the Cabinet of the Chiefs of Staff, was replaced. His parting salvo, quoted above, was fired in the House of Commons and everyone serving in the Commandos in October 1941 heartily agreed with every word he said. For most of them their months in the Commandos seemed in retrospect to have been one long story of hope deferred. In the early days, during that glorious summer when invasion still threatened England, they had been happy enough. Most of the officers had gone to Lochailort in the Western Highlands where they had been instructed in sophisticated methods. of slaughter, and in the art of living off the country. Troops had trained hard in the endeavour to achieve not only perfection but originality; to get away from the tactical legacy of 1914-18 and trench warfare.

In the fall of 1940 five of the Commandos and many assault ships had been concentrated at Inveraray, in preparation for a big operation, the capture of the Azores, which after seemingly endless exercises was cancelled. Next Sir Roger selected Pantelleria as his objective and concentrated his force in the Isle of Arran. This scheme was also cancelled and it cannot be denied that this had an adverse effect on the morale and discipline of at least some troops, but the commander of the Special Service Brigade, Brigadier J C Haydon, DSO, was ready with exhortations adequate to the occasion, and was soon able to revive the original sense of purpose:

'A great enthusiasm at the beginning has evaporated, or at least decreased, owing to the repeated postponements of expected events and enterprises. There is a growing irritation with life . . . this is due partly to these postponements and partly to being harried from pillar to post, on to ships and off them, into billets and out of them, and so on. There is, in short, a sense of frustration.'

The remedy lay with the officers, the best of whom bent all their ingenuity and enthusiasm to devising fresh exercises, tests and techniques, so as to perfect the battle-craft of their men.

In reviving the spirit of his brigade Haydon was helped by three factors. The first was the departure for the Middle East of 'Layforce', whose exploits will be described in the next chapter. The second was the reorganization of the Commandos into a headquarters and six troops, instead of ten. Since this meant that each unit would now have twelve fewer officers, commanding officers had a fairly painless way of getting rid of some of their misfits. The new organization was very much handier from the tactical point of view. Each troop was now to consist of three officers and sixty-two other ranks.

The third factor was the first Lofoten Islands raid. On 21st February the troops embarked at Gourock in the infantry landing ships *Queen Emma* and *Princess Beatrix*, converted cross-Channel steamers. That evening they sailed for Scapa Flow, which was reached next day. A week was spent putting the finishing touches to the planning and training and on 1st March came the signal 'Carry out Operation Claymore'. At midnight the force sailed for Skaalefjord in the Faroe Islands, arriving at 1900 hours on the 2nd. There the five escorting destroyers refuelled and five hours later the expedition sailed again, entering the Westfjord on the night of 3rd March. By 0400 hours next morning the many navigation lights in the vicinity of the Lofotens could be clearly seen. There had been no sign of an enemy. Everything was going

Admiral of the Fleet Sir Roger Keyes

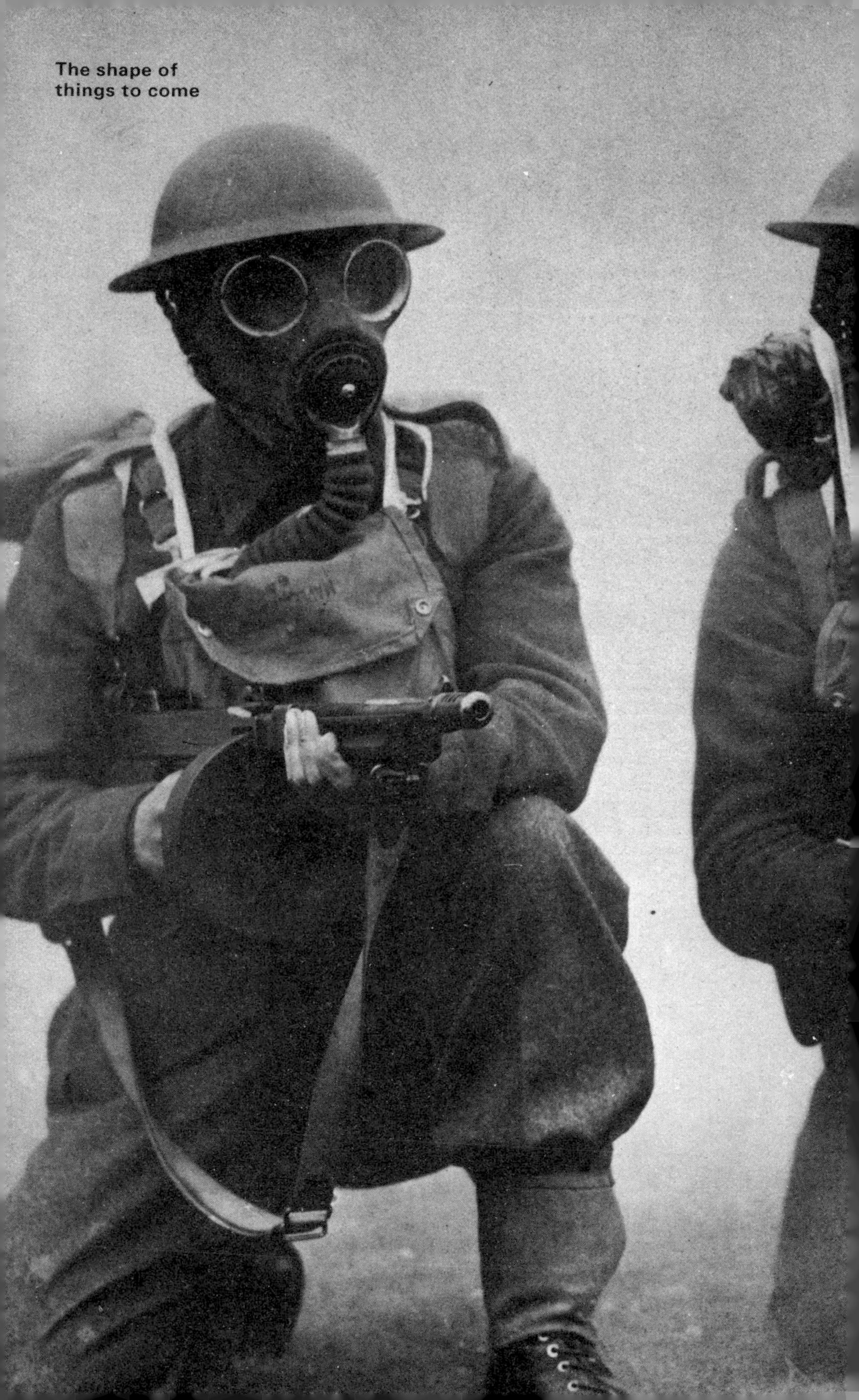

The shape of
things to come

Left, above and below: Crossing obstacles in training. *Below:* Major-General J C Haydon (then Major) the man who trained the Commandos. *Bottom:* HMS Queen Emma, an infantry assault ship with an LCA at the davits

Above: The Lofoten Islands off the coast of Norway, scene of two Commando attacks in 1941

Above: The raid on Vaagsö, 27th December 1941, had similar aims to the earlier Lofoten raid, but was carried out by more men, and involved the temporary occupation of Maalöy Island. *Left:* Western Europe and Mediterranean, the area over which Hitler could expect Commando raids to occur, with a consequent need to keep troops who might be more profitably employed elsewhere in Europe as garrisons and guards

to plan. This perfect landfall was assisted by the submarine *Sunfish*, which acted as a navigational beacon.

Away to the southward a powerful covering force under no less a person than the Commander-in-Chief, Home Fleet, was hoping that some major German warship would have the temerity to interfere with the proceedings. This force included HMS *Nelson*, *King George V*, *Nigeria*, *Dido* and five destroyers.

The objects of the raid were to destroy fish-oil factories so as to deprive the Germans of glycerine for the manufacture of explosives; to sink enemy shipping; to enlist volunteers for the Norwegian forces in the United Kingdom, and to capture supporters of the traitor, Vidkun Quisling. The ports of Stamsund and Henningsvaer were allotted to Number 3 Commando; Svolvaer and Brettesnes to Number 4. The military force was under the

The Lofoten Islands raid

command of Brigadier Haydon. Detachments of the Royal Engineers and of Norwegian soldiers were with each Commando.

Needless to say officers and men had eagerly devoured every scrap of available information, for few indeed had even so much as heard of the Lofoten Islands previously. The nearest big German garrison was sixty miles away at Bodo, while there was another at Narvik, a distance of one hundred miles. There were posts of twenty men in some of the islands, but none were reported at Stamsund or Svolvaer. A U-Boat had been seen in Narvik in January, but, though armed trawlers escorted the coastal convoys, no other warships were known to be in the area. There were usually some German soldiers aboard the mail steamer which was thought to visit the islands daily.

In March the airfields as far south as Trondheim, 300 miles away, were unfit for aircraft not fitted with skis, and so, for once, the threat from the

Luftwaffe was not a major factor – a considerable luxury at that stage of the war!

Soon after 0600 hours the landing craft began their run in. The sun rose bright as they headed for the snow-clad islands, but the air was chill and the blunt-nosed landing craft slapping the choppy sea sent icy spray over the soldiers. One officer whose 'uniform' included two vests, two pullovers, a shirt, a waistcoat, and a wool-lined mackintosh and fur-lined boots complained afterwards: 'I was still cold'.

As Durnford-Slater, well ahead in Number 3 Commando's leading craft, approached Stamsund he met a Norwegian fishing fleet coming out. 'Hvor ar Tuska?' ('Where are the Germans?'), the officers shouted and were somewhat crestfallen to have it confirmed that there were none. The Norwegians for their part hoisted the national colours, which had been flying at half-mast, to the masthead.

The landing at Stamsund proved something of an anti-climax. The 'gently shelving beach' turned out to be a high quay, and the stormers found themselves hauled bodily ashore by the inhabitants who had flocked down to greet them, tying up the landing craft and handing the weapons ashore. After this somewhat un-military beginning the Commando fanned out and lost no time in seizing its objectives. Then the work of destruction began.

The only opposition came from the German armed trawler *Krebbs* which very gallantly took on the destroyer HMS *Somali*, but was set on fire and compelled to surrender.

The results of the raid were highly satisfactory. The volunteers taken off numbered 315, including eight women and one soldier, who emerged from his home in full Norwegian uniform, rifle in hand, accoutred just as he had been when the fighting ended in 1940. The English manager of Allen and Hanbury's factory was rescued from Henningsvaer. German prisoners, mostly Luftwaffe personnel taken by Number 4 Commando, totalled 216. In addition the Norwegian detachment rounded up some sixty Quislings.

Eleven ships with a total tonnage of more than 20,000 tons were sunk, while one trawler was manned and taken back to England. Eighteen factories were destroyed and it is estimated that 800,000 gallons of oil and petrol were burned. The film of all this taking place was an effective piece of war propaganda at a time when there was no surfeit of Allied successes. The only British casualty is thought to have been an officer who succeeded in shooting himself with his Colt automatic, which he had stuck in a trouser's pocket.

The raid had its lighter side. One sergeant, who had been issued with one hundred Kroner for use in the event of his being left behind and having to make his way to neutral Sweden, could only account for seventy when he returned aboard. It transpired that he had found time to bestow the other thirty on a nubile young Norwegian girl whilst ashore. He was known ever after as 'Thirty Kroner So-and-So', but his name shall not be revealed here.

John Durnford-Slater made a memorable harangue to a number of suspected Quislings before departing. He always spoke in a rather breathless, high-pitched voice. Now, speaking with great rapidity, he said: 'Yeah, well, I don't want to hear any more of this bloody Quisling business. It's no bloody good, I'm telling you. If I hear there's been any more of it, I'll be back again and next time I'll take the whole bloody lot of you. Now clear off'.

Small wonder if they departed looking somewhat bemused. Perhaps they were trying to translate the strange English word 'Quisling-business'.

In 1955 Charley Head, who had been Adjutant of Number 3 Commando, revisited the islands, and learned that the Germans had arrived on 5th March and burned a few houses, but they had not shot any of the inhabitants who had welcomed the Commandos so warmly. On the island of Svolvaer, where Number 4 Commando had landed, stands a memorial to eight of the volunteers who had sailed for England in the *Princess Beatrix*. Seven

Demolition party regard their handiwork

Left: German wounded being transferred to hospital ship.
Right: German prisoners and Quislings

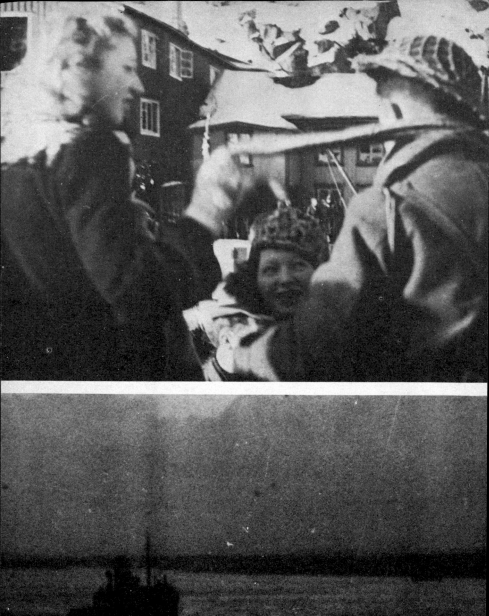

Top left: A fond farewell. *Top right:* Mr Hawes, a Naval officer, and Lieutenant-Colonel Durnford-Slater after the raid. *Above:* The return home.

Spitzbergen

had lost their lives serving with the Royal Navy and one with the Norwegian Troop of Number 10 (Inter-Allied) Commando.

The next important amphibious expedition was not strictly speaking a Commando raid, for the main body of the military force involved was a detachment of Canadian troops under Brigadier A E Potts. Nevertheless it requires mention here as part of the story of Combined Operations. This was the landing in Spitzbergen, 350 miles from the northern point of Norway. The object was to disable the coal mines in order to deny their produce to the Germans.

Once again there was no opposition. The inhabitants were evacuated, the Russians to the USSR, and the Norwegians to the United Kingdom. 450,000 tons of coal were set on fire as well as 275,000 gallons of fuel oil, petrol and grease.

The Germans only learned of the raid when the force was on its way home. On the night 3rd/4th September the wireless station at Tromsoe could be heard trying to get Spitzbergen on the air – in vain.

The Spitzbergen Raid. *Below:* **Canadian Soldiers outside the Communal building.** *Right:* **Fuel dumps on fire at Barentsberg**

This was the last large-scale operation of the period when Sir Roger Keyes was Director of Combined Operations. There were a few minor raids on the French coast, carried out by men of Numbers 2, 5, 9 and 12 Commandos, but it cannot be claimed that any of them did any damage worthy of Hitler's notice. In war the mind of the enemy commander is the ultimate objective and any raiding that had taken place so far had attracted his attention to his Norwegian rather than his French front. For various reasons, including the range of fighter cover, the coasts of Denmark, Germany, Holland and Belgium were not really vulnerable to raiding.

On 27th October 1941 the Lord Louis Mountbatten, GCVO, DSO, ADC, succeeded Sir Roger Keyes as Director of Combined Operations. He was promoted Commodore, First Class. It was a brilliant choice, for which the credit is due to Winston Churchill himself. Mountbatten was a man of forty-one. He had made a tremendous name for himself in command of the destroyer *Kelly*, which, after a splendid fighting career had been sunk off Crete earlier in the year.

H St George Saunders wrote in 'The Green Beret': 'The successor of Keyes was a man of boundless energy and

Left: **Lord Louis Mountbatten.**
Above: **On the polo field**

determination. Lord Louis Mountbatten, a cousin of the King, had spent all his active life in the Royal Navy. In the twenties he had seemed to those who did not know him to be a good-looking naval officer married to a beautiful and wealthy woman, who concerned himself more with the pleasures of life than with its responsibilities. He owned a flat which was the wonder of Mayfair; he played polo; he frequented all the fashionable resorts; he was a hedonist. Nothing, in fact, was further from the truth. These were but the outward signs of a temperament which led him, as it still does, to embrace life with a wide gesture while at the same time being well aware that cakes and ale are but the trimmings of the banquet. Those who knew him well were impressed by the seriousness of purpose which remains the mainspring of his character . . .

The discerning eye of the Prime Minister had long had him in view. He had energy, brains, and determination of the highest order, all qualities in which a Chief of Combined Operations must excel. To these, as well as to his youth, his vigour, and his frank personality, he owed his appointment.'

Sir Roger Keyes was a fire-eater if ever there was one, and the hero of Zeebrugge was greatly admired by the Commando men, whom he tried to launch against the enemy. Even so he was a remote, almost historic figure. In Mountbatten the Commandos found a leader of their own generation. And in one respect Keyes seems to have been seriously at fault. Frustrated by the Chiefs of Staff and by shortages of weapons and landing craft, he had abandoned the realistic policy of launching frequent small scale raids and had attempted to mount operations on a brigade-group scale. The capture of Pantelleria, on which he set his heart, could have done the Allies no good in the early days of 1941. Had he landed 4,000 Commandos there they would have been scarcely more useful than a similar number incarcerated in a German POW camp. It seems that he thought that if his 4,000 men were idle long enough the 'powers that be' would eventually be stirred to action. As he revealed in his parting shots, he underrated Whitehall's capacity for procrastination.

But a new day was dawning.

The adventures of Layforce

'The Commando soldier ... apt à tout'

In February 1941 a considerable detachment from the Special Service Brigade was sent to the Middle East. It consisted of Numbers 7, 8 and 11 Commandos and sailed in the assault ships HMS *Glenroy*, *Glengyle* and *Glenearn*.

In command was Lieutenant-Colonel R E Laycock and a better choice could not have been made. Bob Laycock was a splendid officer, tough and resolute. As befitted an officer of the Royal Horse Guards he demanded the highest standards of courage, initiative and discipline, and in these respects he himself set an unswerving example. To his great qualities of character and personality must be added a thorough professional equipment. He was one of the few senior officers of the Commandos who had had the benefit of a course at the Staff College. Indeed this qualification had nearly curtailed his raiding career before it had begun. When he left Camberley in 1940 he was supposed to go as Anti-Gas Staff Officer to General Headquarters, Middle East. It was not

a role to appeal to a thruster, and being determined to get command of one of the Commandos, he lost no time in finding a substitute. And so it came to pass that when Bob Laycock eventually turned up in the Middle East it was not as a Grade III Staff Officer but as the commander of a formidable brigade.

On arrival two small Commandos, 50 and 52, which had been locally raised and recently amalgamated into one, were added to his command. Layforce now became a brigade of the 6th Division of General Wavell's Army and the Commandos were renamed. Number 7 became 'A' Battalion; Number 8, 'B'; Number 11, 'C'; and the Combined (Middle East) Commando, 'D'.

Layforce arrived in Egypt at a time when Rommel's first onslaught in the desert had wrested the initiative from the British. The situation was further complicated by the German attack on Yugoslavia on 6th April, which was followed soon after by the invasion of Greece.

Major-General R E Laycock

Laycock was eager to prove the worth of his as yet untried units, and in April he was ordered to mount a raid on the port of Bardia, in Cyrenaica, which after being captured during General O'Connor's offensive on 5th January 1941 had recently been retaken by Axis forces. The object was to harass the enemy's lines of communication and to inflict damage on his supplies and war material. One complication was that the port was outside the range of fighter cover.

HMS *Glengyle* with 'A' Battalion Commando aboard set sail on the night 19th/20th April, escorted by the anti-aircraft cruiser HMS *Coventry* and the three Australian destroyers, HMAS *Stuart*, *Voyager* and *Waterhen*. HM Submarine *Triumph* was to take up a position two and a half miles off Bardia, and show a white light as a navigational aid. Unfortunately she was attacked by aircraft during her passage and delayed. The aircraft were British.

Below: **Bardia; a forbidding coastline.**
Bottom: **HMS Glengyle**
Below right: **Major-General Bernard Freyberg VC, the defender of Crete**

Captain Courtney of the Folboat Troop (Special Boat Section) was supposed to show a green light from an offshore islet, but his folboat was wrecked by the heavy swell as he was launching it from *Triumph's* conning tower. Thus the navigational lights which *Glengyle* counted upon did not appear. However she reached the correct position and launched her landing craft at 2235 hours. Owing to trouble with the release gear they began their run in fifteen minutes late, but most of them touched down more or less on time.

There were four beaches. At 'A', the most northerly, the men landed without difficulty, wading ashore in two feet of water. They were joined by the men who were meant to land at 'B'. They had been delayed when their craft stuck in the falls and had joined the flotilla steering for 'A'. The senior army officer pointed out the mistake but his sailor knew better. At 'C' the landing party were late. At 'D', though the approach was narrow and difficult, thirty-five men waded ashore through the swell within ten minutes of the right time

All the landings had been unopposed, and indeed except for two motor-cycle patrols and a couple of lorries there were few enemy about. Men from 'A' beach hurled bombs at these last, but they fell short. An officer moving from one party to another failed to give the countersign when challenged, and was shot and mortally wounded. They discovered a dump of tyres which they set on fire with four incendiary bombs. With this they had to be content, and though it burned fiercely for some hours it was not much of an exploit. Some of the men withdrew to 'B' beach found no landing craft there, and a number were taken prisoner.

The men from 'C' beach damaged a bridge, but their explosives made little impression on the road. Their main objective was a pumping station, but they found it so late that they had no time to demolish it.

The men from 'D' beach found four naval guns. Corporal Baxford and Sapper Angus blew up their breaches with gelignite.

The compasses in the assault landing craft proved defective, which compli-cated the withdrawal, but the *Glen-gyle* got back safely to Alexandria at 2300 hours on the 30th.

The raid was a disappointment. The men, most of whom had not been in action before, had moved far too slowly. This was partly because they were afraid of making too much noise, and partly because they tended to take cover as soon as anyone opened fire. More experienced troops might have known that fast moving men are not much of a target in the dark. But if Laycock was ill-content with this performance the Germans were suffici-ently alarmed to pull back an armour-ed brigade from Sollum.

Further raids on Rommel's com-munications might have paid divid-ends, but the enemy air force now had the upper hand, and no warship slower than a destroyer could have carried out a raid with any chance of survival. Moreover so many troops had been sent to Greece that Layforce was now practically Wavell's only general reserve. Number 11 Commando had to be sent to Cyprus whose garrison seemed dangerously weak.

By 2nd May the British had been driven out of Greece and eighteen days

later the Germans invaded Crete. The inadequate garrison was commanded by a great fighting soldier, Major-General Freyberg VC, who was determined that his men should give a good account of themselves. For a time the unequal struggle hung in the balance and Layforce was sent as a reinforcement. On 25th May Laycock tried to land at Sphakia but was foiled by bad weather and had to return to Alexandria. Transhipped to the fast minelayer HMS *Abdiel* he returned immediately and managed to land in Suda Bay on the night 26th/27th May. When dawn broke Layforce was holding a defensive position astride the main road inland from Sphakia. Here they were heavily dive-bombed, an ordeal which the men endured with fortitude. Captain Evelyn Waugh, the novelist, an old friend of Bob Laycock's was serving as one of his staff officers. A man of cool, almost insolent courage he delivered himself of this opinion: 'Like all things German it is very efficient, but it goes on much too long.'

By the 28th it was clear that the battle was lost, and that once more the Royal Navy was faced with the task of getting the Army away. It fell to Layforce to cover the retreat. On that day Captain F R J Nicholls led G Troop in a bayonet charge which drove the Germans from a hill enfilading Number 7 Commando's position. It does not fall to everyone to lead a charge with the cold steel. It is an exhilarating experience, as Nicholls revealed when he wrote home a few days later: 'One thing I am certain about after Crete is that, man for man, there is not any question as to who is the better. Although they [the Germans] had every advantage of air support, etc., whenever they counterattacked or got to close quarters, which in our own case was twice, they dropped their weapons and fled before us – a very heartening sight.'

It is sad to have to record that this splendid officer was afterwards killed in Burma.

Laycock, no mean tactician, was not slow to discover the way to fight a rearguard action in the teeth of the Germans. Just before dark he would launch a few light counter attacks, no more than fighting patrols of seven or eight men. This sufficed to keep the Germans quiet for the night – they like their sleep. Even so it was a time of chaos and confusion; a retreat has a nightmare quality that is difficult to describe. Units hard hit and short of officers begin to fall apart, rumour is rife, and an iron hand is needed to keep the sleepy, hungry soldiers from despair. Laycock was equal to the worst the Germans could devise. On the 28th his headquarters, which chanced to have three tanks with it, was ambushed. What followed is best described in his own words: 'By the most fortunate chance the ambush was close to the three tanks and the Germans did not see them. The enemy were about thirty yards or less away from us when my Brigade Major and I jumped into a tank and drove straight over the Germans.'

Thus lightly he dismissed this exploit, but how many brigade commanders in any army can drive a tank at all, let alone leap into one and counterattack on the spur of the moment?

In Crete it needed men of this calibre to keep the men going. The troops of the original garrison were exhausted, footsore and thirsty. The Commando men were no better off. A gallant sergeant, Charles Stewart, recalled that when eventually his men got some rations they ate them 'as quietly as a female pig after suckling her young.' Eventually the Commandos reached the beach at Sphakia only to find that there were hardly any craft to take them off. Stewart, in order to help two wounded comrades, gave up his own chance of escape. One party got back to North Africa under sail in a landing craft, which had run out of fuel. The sail was made of blankets lashed together with bootlaces and the voyage took six days. It is fitting that the name of the Royal Marines, who commanded this unlikely odyssey should be remembered.

The Commando soldier was always ready to turn his hand to anything – *apt a tout* as the old French cavalry put it. All the same they were ill-equipped and too lightly armed for the task they were asked to perform in Crete. If they did their job, and

Reception committee: Stukas dive-bombing British shipping in Suda Bay

The disadvantage of not having air
cover. Another view of Suda Bay.

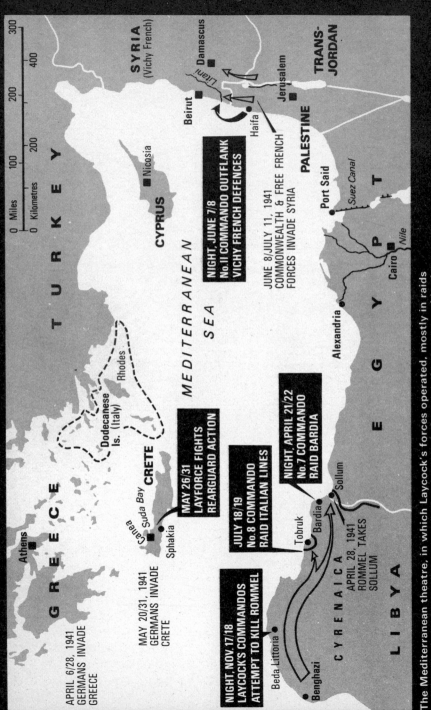

The Mediterranean theatre, in which Laycock's forces operated, mostly in raids behind the German lines in North Africa, although Commandos were used in the

they certainly did, it was because, inspired by a determined leader, they rose above their purely physical disadvantages. Their casualties numbered some 600 – three-quarters of the force that had landed at Suda Bay.

On 8th June the British were compelled to invade Syria where General Dentz, the French High Commissioner, had permitted the Italians to establish air bases. Australian troops advancing north from Palestine were held up near the mouth of the Litani River. To unlock this line it was decided to land Number 11 Commando, which it will be recalled had been in Cyprus when the rest of Layforce was in Crete. The objective was a strong redoubt covering the bridge at Kafr Bada, the bulk of whose garrison belonged to the 22nd Algerian *Tirailleurs*.

The Commando embarked at Haifa in HMS *Glengyle*, commanded by Captain C H Petrie, RN. The landing was not likely to be an easy one. In summer the mouth of the Litani River is usually closed, and owing to the lie of the land it is extremely difficult to identify from the sea. Moreover there is usually a good deal of surf along the Syrian coast, which makes a landing practically impossible on most nights of the month. Fortunately Captain Petrie had discovered in Haifa a young officer who had served in the Palestine Police. This was Sub-Lietenant F H Colenut, RNVR, a man of courage and resource, who landed on the night 6th/7th June and reconnoitred the beaches. On the strength of his report it was decided to carry out the operation on the following night, landing the Commando in three groups north of the river so as to take the defenders in flank and rear. The left group was to be commanded by Captain George More; the centre by Lieutenant-Colonel R R H Pedder; and the right by Major Geoffrey Keyes.

It had been full moon on the previous night and so the landing craft, which were launched just before dawn, had to run in with the setting moon behind them and the rising sun ahead. Even so they had an unopposed landing, though Keyes's group was put ashore to the south of the river. Peering through the twilight they saw what seemed to be a body of troops, but it turned out to be a cypress grove; the troops dashed ashore and cleared the beach. After a time Keyes realized that he had been landed on the wrong side of the river. He lost no time in getting in touch with an Australian battalion from whom he borrowed a boat. In this he ferried his men across the Litani, in the teeth of heavy fire. Thus the Commandos found themselves tackling the very obstacle that their landing was intended to outflank. Keyes was an officer of the Scots Greys and his troop had been selected from famous cavalry regiments. Here his 'cavaliers' as he called them suffered severely, but they got across, where the Australians, no mean fighting men, had failed.

Dick Pedder, a man of fiery temper, was quick to deliver a blistering rebuke if something displeased him. His group pushed inland with vigour and was soon in action. He was in the act of giving orders to some of his officers when a rifle shot hit him in the head, killing him instantly. The other officers were all wounded, but RSM Fraser took command and led the men forward to take the local barracks and a number of men who were about to reinforce the key redoubt.

Further north George More's group had attacked the French gun line, taking a number of field guns and howitzers; the Commandos were actually outnumbered by their prisoners.

Nevertheless the 22nd *Tirailleurs* had not thrown up the sponge. They still had the support of 4-inch mortars, and they had recovered from their initial surprise. Things were looking pretty black for the two northernmost groups of 11 Commando, when about midday the gallant Keyes came on the scene. Taking command, he quickly reorganized the men, and by 1300 hours the redoubt was in his hands.

It was a cruel fate that decreed that Number 11 Commando's first action should be fought against Frenchmen, and in this bitter action the unit suffered 123 casualties, about a quarter of its strength. Both Major Keyes and Captain More were awarded the Military Cross.

From March to December 1941 Rommel's forces besieged Tobruk, which was resolutely defended by a garrison of Australians and others under General Morshead. In this defence a small detachment of five officers and seventy other ranks of Number 8 Commando played their part, sharing the dangers and hardships of the siege, the worst of which, according to Sergeant Dickason, was the shortage of beer. Their chief exploit was a well planned raid carried out by Captain Mike Keely of the Devonshire Regiment.

The objective was an Italian strongpoint called the Twin Pimples, two small hills overlooking the forward defensive positions of the 18th Indian Cavalry. Before the raid the Commandos familiarised themselves with the terrain by going out on patrol with the Indian cavalrymen, who were adept at night movement.

The raiding party comprised forty men of Number 8 Commando and a demolition party of Australian sappers. Keely had with him two excellent officers: Captain Philip Dunne (Royal Horse Guards), a skilful and original tactician, who had once been a Member of Parliament, and Lieutenant Jock Lewis (Welsh Guards), who before the war had been a well-known amateur jockey.

Most of Number 8 Commando were Guardsmen, picked for their powerful physique. Half Keely's party were armed with rifle and bayonet, the rest with Tommy guns. All carried hand grenades, and a third of them had groundsheets to use as stretchers. These were rolled up and worn over the shoulder like a bandolier.

They set off, walking briskly, at 2300 hours on the night of 18th July. 'It was like an English summer evening and very pleasant', wrote Philip Dunne. 'We moved in complete silence, being particularly careful not to betray ourselves by coughing. We were all wearing rubber boots. We went through the Italian forward positions and then through their main defensive lines. I shall never know if they were manned or not because we heard nothing from them and were very careful to make no noise.'

They reached the track by which the Italians brought up their rations, turned to the right and got in the rear of the Pimples. As they approached the 18th Cavalry staged a diversion and the Italians began putting up flares and firing at the Indian position.

While the Italians were busily engaged to their front the Commandos were nearing their rear. They were not challenged until they were thirty yards from the position, then they charged in firing from the hip and shouting their password: 'Jock'. The fight only lasted three or four minutes. Keely was seen to charge a machine-gun nest, clouting the crew with the butt of his Tommy gun. According to Sergeant Dickason: 'his Tommy gun was rendered useless, but so were the enemy gunners'. The Italians took cover in their dugouts and the Commandos bombed them out with Mills grenades. Before the raiders withdrew the Australian sappers blew up the Italian ammunition dump and some mortars. It was all over inside a quarter of an hour, and at a cost of one man mortally wounded and four others wounded. The raiders were no more than one hundred yards on their way home when the Italian artillery brought down defensive fire and began to plaster the Twin Pimples. In planning the raid it was reckoned that it would take them fifteen minutes to realize what was going on, a nice piece of calculation in a thoroughly well planned and executed operation.

After the Litani river Number 11 Commando had returned to Cyprus, but what remained of the rest of Layforce was concentrated near Alexandria. Replacements for the men lost in Crete and Syria were not forthcoming and it was reluctantly decided to disband the force. Most of the men returned to their units, but a few went with David Stirling, Jock Lewis, and Paddy Mayne to form the Special Air Service, and to write a new chapter in the history of raiding.

A small force, which was designed to wage amphibious warfare in the Mediterranean, remained under Laycock's command. It was with these men that he made his daring attempt to turn the course of the war by eliminating the Desert Fox himself.

Laycock himself was in overall command of the operation while Lieutenant-Colonel Keyes had asked to lead the actual assault on Rommel's Headquarters at Beda Littoria. The objective laid down by the Eighth

Lieutenant-Colonel Geoffrey Keyes VC

Army, under whose operational command the group came, was to kill or capture the German general. The raid was to take place at midnight on 17th/18th November and was to coincide with the opening of General Auchinleck's offensive to relieve Tobruk. It involved landing far behind the enemy lines.

Laycock did not conceal from his followers that he considered the raid extremely hazardous. The attack on Rommel's house, he thought, meant almost certain death for the assault party. Moreover, as he frankly pointed out, 'the chances of being evacuated after the operation were very slender.' The soldiers were quite unmoved by these realistic, if gloomy, forebodings, while Keyes for his part urged Laycock not to repeat them lest the 'powers that be' should cancel the whole show.

The force sailed from Alexandria on 10th November in the submarines *Torbay* and *Talisman*. The British soldier loves novelty and the men,

Below: HMS Torbay. *Bottom:* HMS Talisman

delighted at this fresh and relatively subtle way of reaching their target, had nothing but praise for their food and accommodation.

Both submarines reached the rendezvous on time, and a torch flashed from the shore signalled that the beach was clear. Disguised as an Arab, Captain J E Haselden, an intrepid Intelligence officer, had been dropped by the Desert Reconnaissance Group to act as a one-man reception committee. A heavy swell rendered the landing excessively hazardous. As Keyes's party were launching their two-man rubber boats from the *Torbay* a large wave swept four of them into the sea with several of the soldiers. Laycock had even more trouble landing from the *Talisman* and most of his boats were capsized. Only half of the two parties eventually struggled ashore and gained the *wadi* where they were to lie up for the day.

The force was now divided into three groups. Laycock with a sergeant and two men was to stay in the *wadi* to look after the dump of ammunition and rations, and to direct the rest of the *Talisman* party if they got ashore next

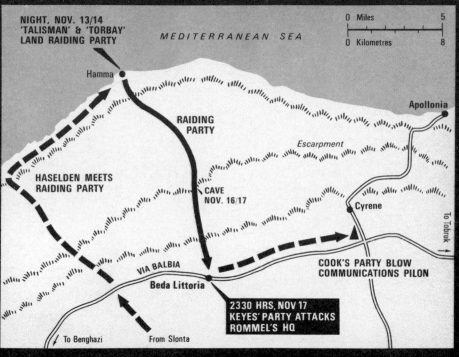

The courageous but unfortunate attack on Rommel's HQ, the *Rommel-haus*.
There were only two survivors from the raiding party.

night. Lieutenant Gay Cook and six men were to cut the telephone and telegraph wires at the crossroads south of Cyrene. Keyes was to lead the actual assault.

The sun dried the men's clothes as they lay in the *wadi*. Once an aircraft, painted with red crosses, flew over, but evidently they were not spotted. In the afternoon it came on to rain.

At 2000 hours Keyes set off. The going, mostly on rock-strewn sheep tracks, was extremely difficult, but dawn found Keyes and his men ensconced on a small hill. Here they were discovered by a party of Arabs armed with Italian carbines. Fortunately the party included Corporal Drori, a Palestinian who spoke perfect Arabic. With him as interpreter Keyes won over their leader, a 'very villainous-looking Arab with a red headcloth wound round his head at a raffish angle'. (From *The Green Beret* by H St George Saunders). At midday the Arabs brought kid's meat and soup, the first hot meal the men had had for thirty-six hours. Keyes was able to buy them some cigarettes with Italian money he had with him.

When it got dark they set out once more, the 'brigand' leading them in about two and a half hours to a large, dry cave with 'an appalling smell of goat'. Here they rested, moving on next morning, since in the bad weather goatherds were likely to shelter in the cave. Their next hide was a small wood, where wild cyclamen grew. Here they breakfasted on 'arbutus berries that look and taste like strawberries and are called by the Senussi the Fruit of God'. Next Keyes set out on a reconnaissance and was able to make out the escarpments near the objective. A thunderstorm came on and he decided to risk returning to the cover of the cave. An Arab boy, who had accompanied the guide, spied out the land in and around Beda Littoria, and from his information Keyes was able to draw 'an excellent sketch map of the house and its surroundings'. With its aid he was able to brief them for the attack, assigning each group the place where it was to deploy. It was a day of thunderstorms and the desert turned to mud. Keyes, making the best of things, pointed out that in the foul weather their approach march was the less likely to be observed.

At 1800 hours on the 17th the raiding party set off in pouring rain to march the last stage of their journey. They were soon soaked, but struggling along in the ankle-deep mud, they had reached the foot of the rocky escarpment by 2230 hours. They had time for a short rest before scaling this obstacle. There was a bad moment half-way up, when they 'roused a watchdog and a stream of light issued from the door of a hut . . . a hundred yards on our flank. As we crouched motionless, hardly breathing, we heard a man shouting at the dog. Finally the door closed'.

They found the track which according to their Arab guides led to the back of Rommel's Headquarters. Here Cook's party set off to carry out its task. The rest began their final approach, Keyes himself and Sergeant Terry acting as scouts and Captain Campbell bringing up the main body fifty yards behind them. When they had gone a quarter of a mile they dropped the guides, impressing upon them that they must await the raiders' return or forfeit their reward. Pushing on, weapons at the ready, at about 2330 hours they reached some outbuildings within one hundred yards of the headquarters house. While Keyes and Terry were making their final reconnaissance a dog began to bark, and an Italian soldier accompanied by an Arab came out of a hut. Campbell told him in German – 'as imperiously as I could' – that they were a German patrol, an assertion which Corporal Drori repeated in Italian. As the soldier turned away Keyes returned, and deployed his men for the assault. Keyes, supported by Campbell and Terry, pushed through a hedge into the garden, round a corner, and was running up a flight of steps to some glass-topped doors when a German officer, in steel helmet and greatcoat, appeared in his path. Campbell describes what followed:

'Geoffrey at once closed with him, covering him with his Tommy gun. The man seized the muzzle of Geoffrey's gun and tried to wrest it from him. Before I or Terry could get round behind him he retreated, still holding on to Geoffrey, to a position with his back to the wall and his

Right: Sergeant J Terry. *Below:* The house in Beda Littoria

German and Italian soldiers at Keyes's funeral

either side protected by the first and second pair of doors at the entrance. Geoffrey could not draw a knife and neither I nor Terry could get round Geoffrey as the doors were in the way, so I shot the man with my .38 revolver which I knew would make less noise than Geoffrey's Tommy gun. Geoffrey then gave the order to use Tommy guns and grenades, since we had to presume that my revolver shot had been heard. We found ourselves in a large hall with a stone floor and stone stairway leading to the upper stories, and with a number of doors opening out of the hall which was very dimly lit. We heard a man in heavy boots clattering down the stairs. As he came to the turn and his feet came in sight, Sergeant Terry fired a burst with his Tommy gun. The man turned and fled away upstairs'.

Keyes threw open a door, but the room was empty. Then, pointing to a light shining under the next door, he flung it open. Inside were something like ten Germans in steel helmets, sitting and standing. Campbell goes on: 'Geoffrey fired two or three rounds with his Colt .45 automatic, and I said: "Wait, I'll throw a grenade in".' Keyes slammed the door shut and held it while Campbell pulled the pin out. 'I said "Right," and Geoffrey opened the door and I threw in the grenade which I saw roll to the middle of the room. "Well Done," said Keyes. A German fired and hit Geoffrey just above the heart'.

He fell unconscious. Campbell shut the door and instantly his grenade 'burst with a shattering explosion'. The light in the room went out, and there was complete silence. Campbell and Terry carried Keyes outside and laid him on the grass by the steps. 'He must have died as we were carrying him outside, for when I felt his heart it had ceased to beat'.

Campbell went back through the hall of the building, and then round to the back entrance, where a Commando soldier took him for a German and shot him. He was badly wounded in the leg. When the soldiers said they would carry him back to the beach, a distance of twenty-five miles, he ordered them to leave him, and it fell to Keyes's devoted follower, Sergeant Terry, to conduct the withdrawal. Soon afterwards the Germans found

Laycock concealed his men in caves with standing patrols watching the flanks. At noon the post to the west was engaged by Arab levies of the Italians. He sent two small parties to outflank these assailants, but some Germans arrived to support the levies, and foiled this move. Pryor, the commander of one of them, was severely wounded, but managed to crawl back. A large party of Italians appeared on the skyline a mile to the north. They did nothing, but by 1400 hours the Germans, keeping up a heavy fire, had closed to within 200 yards of the caves. Laycock now broke his force up into small parties and ordered them to dash across the open and take cover among the hills inland. They were to try and get in touch with the *Talisman*, or to hide in the *wadis* until our own forces should overrun the area. Pryor was left behind with a medical orderly. He was captured and led off on a mule watched 'by a lovely red-backed shrike sitting on a juniper bush.' (From *The Green Beret* by H St George Saunders.)

Bob Laycock and Sergeant Terry ran the gauntlet of continual sniping till they reached the thick scrub of the Jebel. Then they set out to join the Eighth Army. The Arabs befriended them, conversing in broken Italian. 'For instance, a Senussi, holding up his five fingers, pointing at us and then drawing his fore-finger across his throat, meant that five of our original raiding party had been murdered by the Arabs and handed over to the Germans'. Sometimes they had to live for as much as two and a half days on berries alone, but though weakened by lack of food, they never lacked water for it rained continuously.

On Christmas Day 1941, forty-one days after they had set out on the raid, they reached the British forces at Cyrene – the only two to get back. 'On joining them we fell upon the marmalade offered to us and polished off a pot each'.

Colonel Laycock flew back to Cairo to report. There he heard that Haydon was to become military adviser to Mountbatten. He was to return to England and take command of the Special Service Brigade.

Campbell and took him to hospital. His leg had to be amputated. The Germans chivalrously accorded Keyes full military honours, and the chaplain of the garrison church at Potsdam conducted the service. For his determined, gallant and skilful leadership in this desperate enterprise he was awarded the Victoria Cross. He had proved himself a worthy son of a fire-eating father.

Ironically enough it proved that Rommel had never lived in the house attacked, which was in fact the headquarters of German and Italian supply services. Rommel himself was nowhere near, for he was in the forward area with his troops.

Terry succeeded in leading the raiders back to Laycock in the *wadi*, but they waited in vain for Cook. It transpired subsequently that he carried out his mission, but had fallen into the hands of the enemy on the way back.

The *Torbay* returned on the night of the 20th and flashed a message in morse, which Laycock could read, saying that the sea was too rough and she would return the next night. A rubber dinghy with food and water was floated ashore.

Vaagso

'Norway is the zone of destiny in this war. I demand unconditional obedience to my commands and directives concerning the defence of this area.' Adolf Hitler January 1942.

With Mountbatten at the helm a new sense of urgency began to pervade the whole Combined Operations organization, for he soon demonstrated a truly remarkable skill in cutting through red-tape. and oiling the wheels of inter-Service cooperation. It took him precisely two months to lay on his first big raid, an operation which was to have a subtle influence on the whole future course of the war. Vaagso was, moreoever, a minor classic of amphibious warfare, a raid which, despite the multitudinous accidents inseparable from warfare, actually went according to plan, in that all the groups into which the force was divided carried out their assigned tasks.

In general the object of the raid was to attack and destroy the German garrison in the little Norwegian port of South Vaagso. From the strategic point of view this was part of the British policy of harassing the Germans. The more troops they employed to defend the coasts of northwest Europe the less they would have to fight in Russia or North Africa. From the tactical point of view the intention was to destroy the garrison, blow up the fish-oil factories, sink shipping, bring Norwegian volunteers to Britain, capture code-books and documents, and round up Quislings.

The garrison was thought to consist of 150 infantry, a tank and one hundred men of the Labour Corps. A four-gun battery on the islet of Maaloy covered Vaags Fjord, as did a two-gun battery on Rugsundo Island. which last was not one of the objectives. There was a mobile battery of 105mm guns at Halsor on the north coast of Vaagso Island, covering the northern entrance to Ulvesund, where German convoys used to form up, and where shipping could be expected, including armed trawlers. The Germans had no other warships in the area.

The Luftwaffe had three airfields in

Rear-Admiral Sir Harold Burrough on the bridge of his flagship

56

Central Norway, which were within range of Vaagso. They were Herdla, Stavanger, and Trondheim. Fighters (Me 109s) from the last two would have to refuel at Herdla if they were to operate over Vaagso.

The joint force commanders were appointed on 6th December. They were Rear-Admiral H M Burrough, CB, and Brigadier J C Haydon. Their headquarters ship was the 6 inch cruiser HMS *Kenya*. The force was to be escorted and supported by four warships from the 17th destroyer flotilla, HMS *Onslow, Oribi, Offa* and *Chiddingfold*. The soldiers were to be landed from the infantry assault ships HMS *Prince Charles* and *Prince Leopold*. HM Submarine *Tuna* was to play the part of navigational beacon, a point of great importance for earlier in the month a raid on Floro, twenty-five miles south of Vaagso, had been foiled simply because the naval commander was uncertain of his landfall.

The force detailed for the landing consisted of fifty-one officers and 525 other ranks under the command of Lieutenant-Colonel J F Durnford-Slater (Number 3 Commando). It consisted of Number 3 Commando; a troop and a half of Number 2 Commando; detachments of Royal Engineers (Number 6 Commando); Royal Army Medical Corps (Number 4 Commando); and Intelligence officers from the War Office and a Press Unit. Men of the Royal Norwegian Army were attached as guides and interpreters.

The Royal Air Force had only two fighter bases within operational range of Vaagso. These were Sumburgh in the Shetland Islands and Wick at the extreme north of Scotland. They were respectively 250 and 400 nautical miles from Vaagso. From these bases the Beaufighters and Blenheim fighters of Numbers 235, 236, 248, 254 and 404 squadrons would just be able to give the expedition a measure of fighter cover. Bombing missions were assigned to Hampdens of 50 Squadron and Blenheim bombers of 110 and 114 Squadrons of Coastal Command.

On 13th December Number 3 Commando embarked and sailed for Scapa, where the raiding force assembled and the final exercises took place. The briefing was as thorough as man could make it. With maps, air photographs and models every single man was shown his task and a variety of possible alternatives: every man was to be sure he understood his role.

Lord Louis Mountbatten appeared for a last minute visit. His pep talk to the assembled troops ended: 'One last thing. When my ship, the destroyer *Kelly*, went down off Crete earlier this year the Germans machine-gunned the survivors in the water. There's absolutely no need to treat them gently on my account. Good luck to you all!'

The men were wildly enthusiastic, and at least one troop commander felt it necessary to impress on his men the need to take prisoners according to the normal usages of war. But though most of them had been at Dunkirk, he need not have worried; brutality and bravery seldom go hand in hand.

At 2115 hours on Christmas Eve the force sailed for Sollum Voe in the Shetlands. A westerly gale, Force 8, was coming in from the Atlantic, and the assault ships with all their top hamper of landing craft were rolling as if they meant to turn turtle. The force reached Sollum Voe, somewhat battered, at 1300 hours on Christmas Day, and the repair parties set to work. *Prince Charles* had shipped about 120 tons of water, and four cabins on C deck had been flooded. *Chiddingfold* was ordered alongside to help her pump out.

The storm had not yet blown itself out, and according to the weather forecast it would be another twelve or eighteen hours before it did so. In view of this and the damage already sustained, Admiral Burrough decided to postpone the raid for twenty-four hours. The Commandos, all too used to operations that got cancelled at the last moment, speculated endlessly as to the reason for this delay. Rumours were rife, perhaps the most imaginative being that the Pope would not like it if there were operations on Christmas Day. And so Captain Butziger's gunners, celebrating round the Christmas tree with which they had decorated one of their barrack huts, got a day's grace.

Next day Number 6 Commando

Above: HMS Kenya. *Below:* HMS Tuna

Pep talk. Lord Louis Mountbatten with soldiers of No 3 Commando before the Vaagso raid

went ashore far to the north at Reine in the Lofoten Islands, an operation which served to some extent to divert the German attention from the more damaging blow that was about to fall on their forces in Central Norway.

At 1600 hours on 26th December the force sailed once more, and with a following sea, but a falling wind, began the last 300 miles of its voyage.

It was still dark as the troops mustered at their boat stations, every man wearing a leather jerkin or a roll-neck sweater in addition to his normal attire. It was bitterly cold. As it grew light the snowclad land ahead could be seen rising sheer out of the sea, with here and there a light twinkling from the few scattered houses. The silent ships steaming towards this rugged shore made a scene of breathtaking beauty. To Captain Michael Denny, Burrough's flag captain, it must have seemed particularly lovely, for he had made a perfect landfall. *Kenya's* asdic received a signal from *Tuna*, whose conning tower was sighted within one minute of the pre-arranged time. As the flotilla made for the entrance of the fjord, clearing Klovning Island and the Skarningerne rocks, Hampdens began to fly in from the west.

'It was a very eerie sensation entering the fjord in absolute silence and very slowly,' wrote Major Robert Henriques, the well-known author, who was serving as Haydon's brigade major. 'I wondered what was going to happen, for it seemed that the ship (HMS *Kenya*) had lost her proper element, that she was no longer a free ship at sea. Occasionally I saw a little hut with a light burning in it and I wondered whether the light would be suddenly switched off, which would mean that the enemy had spotted us, or whether it would continue to burn as some Norwegian fisherman got out of bed, stretched himself and went off to his nets.

'As we entered the fjord the naval commander gave the order "Hoist the battle ensign!" By tradition the navy then hands down its normal white ensign and replaces it with a thing the size of a double sheet to give the enemy something to shoot at'.

As the landing-craft were lowered the Hampdens attacked Rugsundo and the soldiers could see the distant tracer mount slowly, and against the dark dawn sky. Suddenly the *Chiddingfold* fired an accidental burst from a Bofors. 'That's given the position away,' muttered the pessimist who is inevitably to be found in even the best of units. At 08.42 hours the landing-craft began to move, up the fjord.

For the German garrison the day's work had already begun. The programme for the men of the infantry platoon in South Vaagso was work on their defensive position at the south end of the town, thus by chance they were already at their alarm post. In a hut on Maaloy an NCO was giving the personnel of the battery a lecture on military courtesy: 'How to behave in the presence of an officer'. Captain Butziger had not yet put in an appearance: he was having a shave. His orderly was cleaning his boots. The telephone rang but he was a man who put first things first: he went on with his polishing. Unable to get any response from the battery the lookout at Husevaagso rang through to the harbour captain's office in South Vaagso, and reported that he had seen what appeared to be seven blacked-out destroyers entering the fjord. A clerk assured him that all was well.

'We are expecting a small convoy this morning. It seems they are a little ahead of schedule'.

'They don't look like merchant ships to me,' the lookout replied, only to be crushed with the suggestion that he was still celebrating Christmas! 'Take care you don't get found drunk on duty!'

So far from being tight, the lookout was a conscientious individual and not lacking in persistence. 'Unidentified warships entering fjord' he wrote on a piece of paper, and handed it to the signal orderly to send by blinker lamp to the naval signal station at Maaloy. The recipient, one Van Soest, does not seem to have been quite so cool as the lookout. He acknowledged the message but then, instead of alerting Butziger, who was not more than 200 yards from him, jumped into a boat and rowed across to tell Leutnant zur See Sebelin, the harbourmaster at South

Vaagso. And all this time the British were coming nearer and nearer.

Soon the last two landing-craft of the port column turned away to run in and land at Hollevik, where there was known to be a German post. Minutes passed. Maaloy hove in sight and on the bridge of HMS *Kenya* Admiral Burrough gave the order. 'Open the line of fire.' It was 08.48 hours.

In the Hagen Hotel, his headquarters, Leutnant Sebelin listened to Van Soest's story.

'Did you notify the battery?'

'No, sir. After all, they are an army battery. This is a naval signal'.

Before Sebelin had time to comment there was a crash and *Kenya's* first salvo landed in the town. Thereafter she was on target, and in the next nine minutes she put something like 450 6-inch shells into an area of 250 square yards. The soldiers in the landing-craft could see pieces of the barrack huts flying through the air. *Onslow* and *Offa* lost no time in adding their contribution. The German infantry in Vaagso jumped into their trenches and wondered when it would be their turn. Out in the fjord they could see two columns of landing-craft moving steadily towards Maaloy at about six knots.

The Commandos in their LCA were wondering how long it would be before the four guns on Maaloy, which they were nearing head-on in a kind of amphibious 'Charge of the Light Brigade', would open up on them. They need not have worried. The covering fire from *Kenya* was more than enough to keep Butziger and most of his men in their bunker.

At 08.57 hours Durnford-Slater in the leading craft of the port column put up ten red Verey lights and as the Hampdens came in to drop smoke bombs on the landing places, *Kenya* ceased fire. There came a sudden calm broken only by a few bursts of light machine gun fire and the skirling of Major Jack Churchill's bagpipes. Standing erect in the leading craft of the starboard column he was playing 'The March of the Cameron Men'.

Durnford-Slater had divided his command into five main groups. The first group, of about fifty men, under Lieutenant R Clement, was to clear Hollevik and act as a reserve. The second group, of about 200 men under Durnford-Slater himself, was to take South Vaagso. The third group, of 105 men under Major Churchill, was to take Maaloy and demolish the Mortenes factory. The fourth group, with sixty-five men under Captain R H Hooper, was to act as a floating reserve in HMS *Kenya*. Lastly, the fifth group, thirty men under Captain D Birney, was to block the road at Rodberg.

Lieutenant Clement carried out his task almost without opposition. The two German marines found at Hollevik were both badly wounded and captured. The other eight men from the post had gone to Vaagso for breakfast. Clement attempted to report the position to Commando HQ by wireless, but failing to make contact, signalled his message to *Kenya* so that it could be relayed to Durnford-Slater, who gave instructions for Clement to move up the coast road and come into reserve in South Vaagso.

By this time group 2 could do with reinforcements. Even as it ran in it was hard hit, not by the infantry dug in near the landing place, but by the second of the Hampdens, which were dropping smoke bombs. The German armed trawler *Fohn*, lying in Ulvesund, hit one engine with a burst of anti-aircraft fire. Seconds later the bombardier released a 60 pound phosporus smoke-bomb which by a strange and most unlikely mischance fell in Lieutenant Arthur Komrower's landing-craft, killing or burning nearly half of 4 Troop. Komrower, himself leaping ashore, was trapped half under the landing craft, which was crushing his leg. The Norwegian captain, Martin Linge, dashed into the icy water and rescued him.

The rest of group 2 surged ashore under the cover of a low cliff. They were soon in action. Lieutenant Bill Lloyd, a swarthy Australian, 'bushwhacked' a section of Germans as they ran forward to man their alarm post. With bullets whining overhead 3 and 4 troops rushed in among the wooden houses and factories of Vaagso. Here they were met by German infantry, who for the most part had

Below: HMS Onslow. *Bottom:* HMS Oribi. *Top right:* A flotilla of lightly armoured assault landing craft. They were designed to carry approximately 35 men with their equipment. *Bottom right:* A destroyer passes between Vaagso and Maaloy

Above: Bren-gunner aboard an LCA heads for Vaagso. The church is in the background. *Left:* The only 3-inch mortar in action. *Right:* Covering fire from a Bren

Left: Captain Algy Forester. *Below:* Fighting in the streets

seen action in the Norwegian campaign of 1940, and fought with tenacity. When Oberleutnant Bremer fell defending his strongpoint, Stabsfeldwebel Lebrenz took over command. In the midst of a hostile population every single German bore a hand. The unit chaplain was among the first to fall. Leutnant Sebelin lost no time in getting a grip on the headquarters personnel and sailors, so as to give the defence a bit of depth.

After about a quarter of an hour's fighting Captain Giles (3 Troop) moving up on the left ran into a large house which the German infantry had turned into a strongpoint. Sniped from the windows his men worked slowly forward, firing short bursts, and dashing across the snow-covered gaps to take cover behind buildings, until at length they were close enough to rush the building. Then Giles, a man of gigantic stature, led a wild charge, they burst through the front door, and stormed through the house hurling grenades into each door they came to. The surviving Germans fled through the back door followed by Giles, who stood an instant silhouetted as he glanced each way to decide his next move. A lurking rifleman shot him at close range, and he died almost at once. About the same time his senior subaltern, Lieutenant Mike Hall, had his left elbow shattered by a bullet and 3 Troop's assault began to run out of steam.

On the right Captain Algy Forrester, a fire-eater who had served in Norway in 1940, led his depleted 4 Troop straight up the main street, throwing grenades into the houses, and firing from the hip with his Tommy gun. 'I shouldn't have liked to have been a German in his path,' was Durnford-Slater's comment. Forrester was a host in himself. He needed to be, for Komrower, valiantly hobbling to his support, had hardly any of his section in action, and the ardent Lloyd, soon after his initial success, had been shot through the neck and dangerously wounded. Meanwhile Sebelin had got a handful of men together and improvised a strongpoint in and around the Ulvesund Hotel. By the time 4 Troop came on the scene the Germans were in position. The place could only be carried by a frontal assault. Forrester pulled the pin from a grenade and dashed for the front door. A German inside fired and he fell forwards, his grenade bursting beneath him. Now the only officer left was the Norwegian, Martin Linge, whose task was to collect such secret documents as he could from the German headquarters. Without hesitation he assumed command of 4 Troop. The men knew him well enough to recognize a real leader, and they followed him in a second assault. As he dashed round the corner of a building, a bullet pierced his chest and he fell dead almost in the doorway of the hotel. And so the second attack on the Ulvesund Hotel ebbed away.

4 Troop now seemed to be practically leaderless, but the hour found the man, one 'Knocker' White of the Queen's Own Royal West Kent Regiment. Although a soldier with considerable experience he was only a full corporal, and there were certainly those present who outranked him. But while the loss of their officers had numbed some of the NCOs, in White it had merely stoked up a sort of fighting fury. Finding that nobody else was doing anything positive he began to rap out an order or two and finding himself being unquestioningly obeyed, he took charge.

It chanced that Number 1 Troop thanks to a piece of private enterprise on the part of Captain Bill Bradley possessed a 3 inch mortar. It cannot be claimed that its crew were well drilled, but though they shrank back and covered their ears every time it went off, they could at least fire it. Sergeant Ramsey now appeared and brought this piece into action at a range that cannot have exceeded one hundred yards. Its first bomb seems to have gone down a chimney in the enemy strongpoint, and is said to have caused thirteen casualties. This lucky shot probably turned the course of the fight. At any rate Corporal White with the survivors of 4 Troop and a handful of Norwegians were able with bomb, Tommy gun and rifle, to overcome the last resistance of the resolutely held but now blazing German strongpoint.

Captain A G Komrower

Back at his command post John Durnford-Slater awaited progress reports with what patience he could muster.

At 1020 hours he sent a signal to *Kenya* reporting that the situation in the northern end of the town was not clear and that he had lost wireless touch with 3 and 4 Troops whose sets had been destroyed. Soon afterwards he followed this with a message: 'Fairly strong opposition being encountered in centre and north of Vaagso.' He requested that the whole of Group 4 should be sent in on Group 2's original landing place. To this

A blazing German storehouse on Maaloy

Brigadier Haydon consented.

By this time the colonel had probably sent for 2 Troop. He also signalled to Major Churchill to send what men he could spare. This done, at about 1030 hours, he went forward to reconnoitre. His old friend and signals officer took it into his head to accompany him. There was a lot of shooting going on, but Durnford-Slater, pistol in hand, walked briskly up the main street, looking neither to right nor left. Though he had been on the Guernsey and Lofoten raids he had not previously been under fire, but he had been a daring horseman before the war. Racing and pigsticking had developed his robust frame and his

Landing under fire

Below: Advancing up the main street of Vaagso. *Right:* Reserve ammunition is brought up the main street

iron nerve. Charley Heed was not exactly the most timorous of men, although a certain tactical discretion led him to say: 'You keep a lookout for snipers on the left, sir, and I'll take the right.'

'Lookout nothing,' snapped John, 'I'm in a hurry.' He reached the Ulvesund Hotel unscathed.

Group 3 deployed swiftly as their four landing-craft touched the rocky ledge of Maaloy. Major Churchill disappeared, sword in hand, into the thick smoke, uttering warlike cries. No braver man fought at Vaagso that day, a gallant man to follow in action, though decidedly conservative in his military ideas. He is the only man who, to the certain knowledge of the present writer, has transfixed a German with an arrow from a longbow – but that is another story.

The two troops, 5 under Captain Sandy Ronald, and 6 under Captain

On Maaloy Island. *Below:* German ammunition on fire. Vaagso town in background. *Right:* At the landing place, a medical orderly treats a minor casualty

Young, negotiated the German wire unopposed. A shell had torn a breach through which 6 Troop passed and nobody trod on a mine. Before the smoke had cleared the empty gun positions had been occupied and white Verey lights were soaring skywards to say 'Here I am'. So far no enemy had shown himself. Now a German soldier appeared, dashing out of the smoke as if heading a counterattack against Number 2 gun site. Three rifle shots rang out. He spun round, screamed, and died. 6 Troop rose and advanced down a slight slope towards the huts. Suddenly a little procession appeared, a German officer and some fifteen unarmed men escorted by Lance-Sergeant George Herbert, MM, and two of his sub-section, Banger Halls and Dick Hughes. This group, fully half the personnel of the battery and its commander Captain Butziger, had been rounded up in the bunker to which they had retired when the first British planes came over.

After this it did not take long to clear the rest of the islet. There was a brief scuffle at the battery office where two Germans were killed, but

the capture of the battery took no more than eight minutes. In fact it was taken so quickly that some of 6 Troop were able to swing round one of the guns (they were Belgian 75s), and engage the *Fohn* before she could get out of range, scoring two hits, but with unfused shells.

Perhaps a dozen men of the battery had fallen during the shelling. The crew of the light ack-ack gun had been killed at their piece, but though empty rounds were found in Number 1 gun site nobody seems to have seen it fire at the landing-craft.

Among the captives were two young women, one Belgian and one Norwegian, who might be described as camp followers.

With the island safely in his hands Major Churchill despatched Captain Ronald to Mortenes, where he landed unopposed and destroyed the factory. 6 Troop's demolition squad under Lieutenant Brandwood proceeded to blow up the guns and destroy all the German installations in the island, including a large store of mines which Butziger had not got round to laying.

At about 1015 hours Jack Churchill

got a message from the colonel asking for reinforcements. Soon afterwards Captain Young and eighteen of his men landed not far from the northeast corner of the cemetery, where they were met by Charley Head, the signals officer.

The colonel was not far away, standing in the middle of the main street, smiling.

'Well, Peter, I am glad to see you.' Briefly he told 6 Troop's commander of the attacks on the Ulvesund Hotel, of the losses among the officers and the splendid leadership of Corporal White. It was evident that the attack had lost its momentum. Most of 1 Troop was busy with demolitions, but part of 2 Troop had come up under a fiery lieutenant, Denis O'Flaherty. They were clearing warehouses on the waterfront. The floating reserve had been summoned and was coming ashore.

The party from 6 Troop moved off to reinforce the attack along the shores of the fjord. At first all went well. The 2 Troop men had accounted for several Germans, though not without loss to themselves, O'Flaherty himself

Major Jack Churchill examines one of the four captured Belgian 75s

being nicked in the shoulder.

Four Germans surrendered when men of 6 and 2 Troops rushed a German storehouse. Then the trouble started. Sergeant Hughes and Trooper Clarke were both shot, the former mortally, and nobody could say where the shooting was coming from. Cramped between the storehouse and a woodpile the party had to get room to reorganize. This meant seizing the Red Warehouse sixty yards ahead across a bare patch of snow. Whether the building was occupied none could tell. The troop commander was about half way across the square when a German soldier appeared in the door and began flinging stick grenades. He missed, and his third grenade failed to go off. When about a dozen Mills bombs had been flung into it, an attempt was made to clear the building, but the Germans were still alive. They had retired into an inner room and as the Commandos came through the door fired on them with their rifles. It was a decided check.

The colonel came up.

'We must get on,' he said, but how to do so without useless casualties was not clear. Eventually some petrol was found, but before the Commandos could set fire to the building Lieutenant O'Flaherty and Trooper Sherington made another desperate attempt to storm it. This time both were badly hit, but recovering themselves with admirable fortitude, succeeded in staggering from the warehouse. Soon afterwards 6 Troop set it on fire, and leaving Lance-Corporal Fyson and another man to watch it, pushed on. When it got stuffy these resolute Germans came out, and walked into a burst of Bren gun fire. They had disdained their chance to surrender.

By this time Captain Hooper with the floating reserve had come ashore and reinforced the attack.

At about this time, 1159 hours to be precise, thirteen Blenheim bombers put in an attack on Herdla aerodrome with 250 pound bombs. One bomber was hit by an 88mm shell and colliding with another, crashed with it into the sea. With more than twenty craters in the runway Herdla was out of action not only for the 27th but for several days to come. Planes from Stavanger and Herdla could no longer intervene in the fighting at Vaagso.

While the Commandos were fighting ashore the destroyers were dealing with the shipping in the fjord.

The *Fohn*, 250 tons, had been detailed to escort a convoy consisting of three ships, which were getting up steam as dawn broke. The *Fohn's* twin Oerlikons, it will be remembered, hit a Hampden with disastrous results to 4 Troop, and was herself pierced by two shells, fired solid, by 6 Troop. With the *Norma* (2,200 tons) and the *Reimer Etzard Fritzen* (3,000 tons) she fled northwards but the flat-bottomed schuyt *Eismeer* (1,000 tons) had not got up steam. She hoisted the Dutch flag, but this ruse did not save her for long. Exchanging fire in an unequal fight with *Onslow* and *Oribi* the German flotilla made off, while Leutnant zur See Lohr tried to get rid of *Fohn's* confidential code books. He was killed by a shell from *Onslow* just as he was about to drop them overboard. All three vessels ran themselves aground and the crew of *Fohn*, armed with rifles, engaged the destroyers from the rocky shore until *Onslow's* gunfire drove them off. Lieutenant-Commander de Costabadie, DSC, veteran of Dunkirk and one of Mountbatten's Planning Staff, boarded *Fohn* and after an exchange of rifle fire with her crew carried off her code books, the major intelligence scoop of the Vaagso raid. They gave the radio call sign of every German vessel in Norway and France besides details of their challenges, countersigns and emergency signals. Moreover, the Germans had no reason to suppose that Lohr had not dropped them, bound in lead into the icy depths of Ulvesund.

The *Eismeer* seemed ripe for capture, but, as de Costabadie approached her in a whaler, the seaman pulling the stroke oar was mortally wounded by a bullet from the town. The party got aboard but were prevented by rifle fire from raising the anchor. Captain Armstrong *(Onslow)*, compelled to admit a stalemate, called back his landing party and sank *Eismeer* by gunfire. Soon after, much to her own crew's surprise, *Onslow* managed to dispose of a German aircraft with an antique 4-inch gun which she had recently had mounted aft. On the 28th Armstrong wrote in his report:

'Yesterday was excellent for a new ship. At one moment we were sinking a merchant vessel with the after 4.7, covering the military with the foremost 4.7, engaging aircraft with a 4 inch, and the close range weapons were covering the landing party against German snipers. Unfortunately there was no torpedo target.'

At 1000 hours *Oribi* had landed Group 5, Captain Birney's half troop from 2 Commando, which had set up an ambush at the hamlet of Rodberg in order to prevent German reinforcements coming south from Halsor. This done, *Oribi* had moved to· assist *Onslow*, and had helped her dispose of the armed tug *Rechtenfleth* (200 tons) and the *Anita L M Russ* (2,800 tons) which came sailing innocently down Ulvesund and made the – literally – fatal error of mistaking the British for German destroyers.

The Halsor battery had been attacked by three Blenheims early in the day, but little damage had been done. The commander, Leutnant

The destruction of a warehouse on the waterfront

Lienkamp, heard heavy firing from South Vaagso, but could not get through on the telephone, perhaps because Sebelin had thrown the telephone orderlies into the fight. The Headquarters of the 181st Division, to which the garrison belonged, did not really know what was going on, though observers on Rugsundo had seen warships and landing craft approach Maaloy. Lienkamp, told rather vaguely to find out what was happening sent out his infantry platoon as a fighting patrol. They had a shooting match with Birney, and lost two men.

The Commandos blew the road before re-embarking, covered by a heavy fire from *Onslow* and *Oribi*. They had no casualties.

In the town the arrival of Hooper's troop had given a new impetus to the attack. Lieutenant G D Black and his section pushed forward to the left of the main road, carrying with it men of 1 and 3 Troops, and driving the Germans before them. Black himself was hit in the forearm by a fleeing German, who swung round and fired a burst with his Schmeisser machine pistol. Asked later what he thought

Above: Sergeant Chitty shepherds prisoners. *Below:* Norwegian refugees embark
Right: Second-Lieutenant O'Flaherty is wounded

of the Schmeisser as a weapon, Black, a Canadian, commented cooly: 'Well, I reckon a two-inch group at a hundred yards isn't too bad.'

Along the main street Colonel Durnford-Slater, with his runners, was still advancing. He came up with 6 Troop as they broke into a large house. There was a motor car outside from which it seemed possible that it was the German commander's billet. For once there was no resistance. A careful research revealed only one German, who lay trembling in bed in an upstairs room. 'Let him be,' said Durnford-Slater. This was undoubtedly Major Schroeder, who had been mortally wounded by a shell-burst at the beginning of the fight and carried off to his quarters. There was suspicious movement in a neighbouring building and some of 6 Troop opened fire from an upper window of Schroeder's billet. It seems not unlikely that the men who brought him there to die had slipped out as 6 Troop broke in the front door.

By this time the 6 Troop party had dwindled to half its original strength, casualties, escorts and messengers having diminished it. Worst of all the commander of another troop had taken it upon himself to order Sergeant Connolly's sub-section to carry some of the dead and wounded back to the beach. Durnford-Slater, however, had collected some of 2 Troop and these with his runners were about equal in numbers to the 6 Troop party, which now advanced and took cover along the bank of a small stream. The colonel led his party forward covered by them, and it was now that a curious episode occurred. A German sailor emerged from a side lane, flung a stick grenade at the colonel, and promptly put his hands up. Durnford-Slater dived into a doorway escaping with minor injuries, but both the orderlies who flanked him were badly hurt.

Sergeant Mills, rifle at the hip, advanced towards the German with purposeful mien.

'Nein, nein' cried the sailor.

'Ja, ja!' said Mills, and shot him.

'Yeah, well, Mills, you shouldn't have done that,' was all the colonel said.

This was practically the end of the fighting. About 1145 hours the colonel held a brief conference in a garden, ordered Captain Bradley (1 Troop) to destroy the Firda Factory and put 6 Troop into a good solid house to act as a 'stop' in case the Germans should counterattack before the demolitions were complete. At 1300 hours, by which time all firing had long since ceased, this party withdrew.

The re-embarkation went without hitch, demolitions continuing almost to the last moment. By 1445 hours the troops were back aboard.

Kenya took a hit from the Rugsundo battery at about midday and *Prince Charles* sustained some damage from a bombing attack as the expedition was putting to sea. *Oribi* had a few minor casualties, and the land force lost twenty killed (of whom six, including Captain Giles, were buried at sea), and fifty-seven wounded. Several aircraft were lost. Not a single British prisoner was taken.

The departing raiders left a fair trail of destruction behind them. Every man of the Maaloy battery was killed or taken, its guns were destroyed, its barracks ruined. A number of factories, including the Firda Factory, were burnt or blown up. So were the telephone exchanges, the Seternes lighthouse, and a number of warehouses. The Germans' only tank, a French one, had been blown up in its garage.

At about 1230 hours *Offa* and *Chiddingfold* had disposed of the armed trawler *Donner* (250 tons) and the *Anhalt* (5,930 tons) off the mouth of the fjord, bringing the total of shipping sunk to 15,630 tons.

On 28th December General Kurt Woytasch, the commander of 181 Division, arrived in South Vaagso to survey the damage. It is not easy to be sure exactly how many men the Germans had lost, for no figures seem to be available for a detachment of twenty-five men, who were in the town for the Christmas holiday. The infantry garrison lost eleven killed, seven wounded, and sixteen missing–mostly captured. The marine detachment lost six. The Halsor platoon had two casualties, and the Rugsundo battery, which had made a considerable nuisance of itself with an old Russian 130mm gun (its other was non-

Above: A group of officers pose on the return voyage. Second from the right, behind the capstan, is Captain Ronald. *Right:* Mr John Nygaardsvold, Norwegian Prime Minister in exile

operational), had lost only one killed and eight wounded. Every man of the Maaloy battery was killed or captured. In all the German casualties must have been somewhere between 110 and 130, excluding those sustained by the crews of the eight ships sunk. One Norwegian civilian was killed and five slightly wounded. The damage to Norwegian property exceeded 5,000,000 Kroner.

Though some seventy volunteers returned to the United Kingdom the Norwegian Government in exile was not at all pleased with the results of the raid. The aged Prime Minister, Mr. Nygaardsvold, expressed his opinion very forcibly:

'Who could be so blind as to delude himself that this effort could have done anything to shorten the ordeal of Norway? Undoubtedly the enemy had been annoyed by he very impudence of the operation lancing deep into the shoreline he sought to secure, but it could have only one result: the Germans would now strengthen their defences, making the ultimate victory even harder to achieve than it would have been if the raid had never taken place'.

In one respect he was quite right. The Germans certainly did build up their defences. But since the Allies had no intention of invading Norway that could only do good.

If Nygaardsvold was ruffled, Hitler was infuriated by the Vaagso raid. Even before the blow fell OKW, the German Headquarters in Berlin, had been concerned about possible operations in Scandinavia now that America was in the war on the Allied side. On Christmas Day a fresh appreciation of the situation in Norway had been ordered.

General von Falkenhorst had taken advantage of this to ask for 12,000 replacements in order to bring his divisions up to strength, and three additional divisions to increase his reserves and give more depth to his defensive layout.

On top of Falkenhorst's report came news of Operations 'Archery' and 'Anklet', their effect reinforced by the mining of the troopship *Kong Ring*, with men going on leave, in the North Sea.

Hitler lost no time in demanding of his military advisers their interpretation of these sinister events. Were the British contemplating a larger landing in Norway in order to menace the German coastal shipping? Before the end of the year Hitler had delivered his own verdict:

'If the British go about things properly, they will attack northern Norway at several points. By means of an all-out attack by their fleet and ground troops they will try to displace us there, take Narvik if possible, and thus exert pressure on Sweden and Finland. This might be of decisive importance for the outcome of the war.

'The German fleet must therefore use all its forces for the defence of Norway. It would be expedient to transfer all battleships and pocket-battleships there for this purpose.'

With *Scharnhorst* and *Gneisenau* bottled up in Brest the admirals hoped the Führer would change his mind, but in mid-January he sent for Grand Admiral Raeder and told him: 'Norway is the zone of destiny in this war. I demand unconditional obedience to my commands and directives concerning the defence of this area.'

Meanwhile a cornucopia was pouring gifts upon Falkenhorst. First his 12,000 replacements arrived, then came 18,000 men organized as fortress battalions. An armoured division was activated in Norway to act as a mobile reserve. Good new German coast defence guns were provided to replace antiques like the Russian and Belgian

Top left: Colonel-General von Falkenhorst. *Top right:* Field-Marshal List during his visit of inspection to Norway, on the deck of a U-Boat in Oslo harbour. *Right:* Germans patrol the shores of a Norwegian fjord

guns which had defended Vaagsfjord on 27th December.

In February 1942 Generalfeldmarshall List, as the Führer's personal representative, made a tour of inspection and on his recommendation three more divisional commands were established in Norway, more coast artillery was sent there, and defensive positions were built up in the interior. The process continued until, on 6th June 1944, the day when the Allies landed in Normandy, the German garrison in Norway was 372,000 strong. One wonders what difference even 100,000 of these might have made to the fighting in France or White Russia. The Germans in Normandy were decidedly short of good infantry.

The battleship *Tirpitz* sailed from the Baltic and reached Norway in safety. Then on 11th February 1942 *Scharnhorst, Gneisenau* and *Prinz Eugen* broke out of Brest and, taking advantage of foul weather, made their desperate dash up the English Channel. In the Straits of Dover *Gneisenau* was so hard hit that she had to put into Kiel, where British bombers holed her again before the month was out. *Scharnhorst*, too, was hit but got through to Norway, where, eventually, she was joined by *Gneisenau*. *Prinz Eugen* reached Trondheim, but a torpedo had taken off her rudder and she was compelled to return to Germany for repairs.

Great was the indignation of the British public when these three ships escaped up Channel, but their concentration in Norwegian waters greatly lightened the Admiralty's task, simply because they were so much easier to watch and to keep out of the North Atlantic. In March and April *Hipper* and *Lützow* joined them.

In the Vaagso raid the British hazarded a small flotilla, the equivalent of a weak battalion and half a dozen squadrons of aircraft. Seldom in the history of warfare have such rewards been gained for so small a stake. *Archery* was the code name of the Vaagso raid. It was not inappropriate: the arrow struck the gold.

Scharnhorst and Gneisenau dash up the Channel. Picture taken from the Prinz Engen

St Nazaire

Anyone who even thinks of doing such a thing deserves the DSO.' A Planner at Combined Operations HQ. 'This is not an ordinary raid, it is an operation of war.' Lord Louis Mountbatten 13th March 1942

St Nazaire has been called the greatest raid of all. It was certainly the most desperate. Its main object was to destroy the great gates of the only dry dock, the Forme Ecluse, on the Atlantic coast of France, which was capable of taking the German battleship *Tirpitz*. A secondary, but still important, aim was to do as much damage as possible to the U-boat bunkers and the docks.

The *Bismarck*, the sister ship of the *Tirpitz*, had been sunk on 27th May 1941 whilst making for St Nazaire. In early 1942 the *Tirpitz* herself was actually in Norwegian waters, but it was suspected from intelligence received that she was preparing for a foray into the Atlantic. The Admiralty, ignorant of the Führer's reactions to the Vaagso raid, was not to know that the Germans were far from contemplating a cruise that would bring the *Tirpitz* anywhere near St Nazaire.

The planning of the operation presented peculiar difficulties. Not only was the target 250 miles from Falmouth, the nearest British port; it was six miles up the River Loire. Moreover there were no beaches.

The military force selected for the raid consisted of Number 2 Commando (Lieutenant-Colonel A C Newman) and demolition parties, eighty strong in all, drawn from Numbers 1, 3, 4, 5, 9 and 12 Commandos. They were trained and led by Captain W H Pritchard, RE.

Planning began in February and there was time for a certain amount of training, which was conducted in conditions of great secrecy. The demolition parties were assembled as though for a course of instruction and, when they had received their specialist training, were concentrated aboard the landing ship *Princess Josephine Charlotte* at Falmouth.

Number 2 Commando, whose cadre had come from the Independent Companies, had now been in existence for nearly two years, and had been thoroughly well trained in night movement, the techniques of sur-

Lieutenant-Colonel Charles Newman VC

mounting all kinds of obstacles at speed, route finding, night firing and all the other skills so vital to the raider. Its commander was a rugged territorial infantry officer, with an original turn of mind. As a climax to its training the force was sent on a trip round the Scilly Isles in motor launches in weather so rough that the hardiest were seasick.

A final examination of air photographs showed four newly installed coast defence gun positions in the middle of the dock area. To deal with these thirty Commando soldiers were added to the force, bringing the total to 265 all ranks. Newman paid a visit to Combined Operations Headquarters in Richmond Terrace on 13th March, and after a final briefing session with Mountbatten and his staff left for Falmouth in a staff car. He reached Tavistock that night and 'spent an uneasy night locked in his hotel bedroom with all the plans'. He had left London in somewhat sombre mood— as well he might—but arriving at Falmouth he found his followers in high spirits, their training nearly completed.

There was still time for a full dress rehearsal, an exercise 'to test the defences' of Devonport dockyard. In this the whole force, except the destroyer *Campbelltown*, took part, while the defenders were reinforced by the local Home Guard. Practically everything went wrong, and the defenders were jubilant.

Meanwhile the cover plan was being developed. The force was called the 10th Anti-Submarine Striking Force, and it was discreetly made known that it was to carry out long-range anti-submarine sweeps, far beyond the Western Approaches. It was rumoured that the force was going overseas, and tropical kit, naval sun helmets and so forth were to be seen being smuggled aboard. How much of all this got back to the Germans cannot be told. The funnels of the destroyer *Campbelltown*, which had a vital part to play, were cut down to make her resemble a German *Möwe* class torpedo boat. The last air photographs received before the expedition set sail showed four torpedo boats of that class, berthed alongside the very spot in the dockyard which Newman had selected

for his Command Post. Commander R E D Ryder, the naval force commander, suggested that Newman's reserve, which was only twelve strong, would be needed to deal with them. Newman was unmoved by this dismal intelligence.

The force left Falmouth on the afternoon of 26th March, sailing at fourteen knots in three columns. The midships column consisted of the Hunt class destroyers HMS *Atherstone* and *Tynedale*, the old American destroyer *Buchanan*, which had been renamed *Campbelltown*, and Motor Gun Boat (MGB) 314. The port and starboard columns were made up of motor launches (MLs). At first the weather was rather rough for the MLs, but the wind fell gradually and the night was calm, hazy and moonlit.

There were only two incidents during the voyage. On the second day out a German U-boat was seen on the surface. *Tynedale* opened fire and depth charges were dropped. The expedition was steering a course for La Pallice but even so Ryder had to make up his mind whether the submarine had signalled the presence of the force. Should he turn back? He did no such thing, and, as is now known, the U-boat had in fact reported only the presence of the destroyers. Presumably the MLs were too low in the water for her lookout to spot. Later some French trawlers were encountered. One, *Le Slack*, was boarded, and though nothing suspicious was discovered, her crew were put aboard the *Atherstone*.

Night fell and at 2000 hours the force hove to, as yet undiscovered, for the HQ staff to transfer to MGB 314. At 2200 hours a light from HM Submarine *Sturgeon*, the navigational beacon, was seen right ahead, and the force, flying German colours, began the run in. MGB 314 was leading, with *Campbelltown* (Lieutenant-Commander S H Beattie) next, then fourteen MLs in two columns, with Motor Torpedo Boat 74 bringing up the rear. Meanwhile bombers of the RAF were attacking St Nazaire through low cloud and the trails of German tracer could be seen mounting skywards.

The expedition had safely negotiated the dangerous mud flats when at 0122 hours searchlights were suddenly

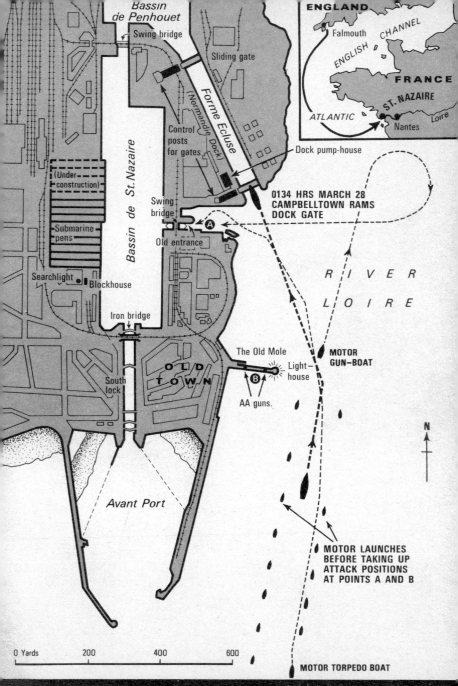

ENGLAND

Falmouth

ENGLISH CHANNEL

FRANCE

ATLANTIC

ST. NAZAIRE

Nantes

Loire

Bassin de Penhouet

Swing bridge

Sliding gate

Forme Ecluse

Normandie Dock

Control posts for gates

Dock pump-house

(Under construction)

Bassin de St. Nazaire

Submarine pens

Swing bridge

Old entrance

0134 HRS MARCH 28
CAMPBELLTOWN RAMS
DOCK GATE

A

Searchlight

Blockhouse

Iron bridge

South lock

OLD TOWN

The Old Mole

Lighthouse

B

AA guns.

R I V E R

L O I R E

**MOTOR
GUN-BOAT**

N

Avant Port

**MOTOR LAUNCHES
BEFORE TAKING UP
ATTACK POSITIONS
AT POINTS A AND B**

0 Yards   200   400   600

MOTOR TORPEDO BOAT

Operation 'Chariot', the raid on St Nazaire on 28th March 1942. The ramming
and destruction of the lock-gates into the dry dock put out of action the only
dry dock outside German waters capable of accommodating the mighty *Tirpitz*.

Left: Commander R E D Ryder VC. *Above:* Lieutenant-Commander R H Beattie VC

switched on from both banks and the force was challenged. Leading Signalman Pike, disguised as a German petty officer, signalled back giving the call sign of a German torpedo boat, learned from *Föhn's* code book taken at Vaagso. He required the shore batteries to wait, adding in plain language, that two craft, damaged by enemy action, requested permission to proceed to harbour without delay. On this the few guns which had already opened up ceased fire, though those on the north bank were not long silent. MGB 314 then made the international signal for ships being fired on by friendly forces.

These ruses, all perfectly legitimate, won the force a good five minutes, and when at 0127 hours the Germans opened up in earnest *Campbelltown* was already past the heaviest batteries. Hauling down her German colours, she ran up the White Ensign and opened fire. Tracer began to fly in all directions, and a German guard ship, hit time and again by both sides, was sunk. The fire of the British flotilla was extremely effective and after three or four minutes the German fire began to slacken. 'A triumph', as Ryder said, 'for the many gunlayers in the coastal craft and in the *Campbelltown.*'

Nothing could stop the old destroyer now, and at 0134 hours, four minutes late, she crashed into the lock gates at nineteen knots. There was a staggering shock as her bows cleaved into the great caissons. The main object of the raid had been achieved before a single Commando soldier had set foot ashore.

Now began a fight of almost incredible complexity, as assault and demolition parties rushed to carry out their varied tasks. In general, Newman's plan was to form a bridgehead and to cut off the approaches to the dockyard area from the rest of the town.

A party under RSM Moss had been detailed to seize Newman's selected Command Post, but the motor launch this group was in was sunk. The RSM struck out for the shore, towing some of his men on a Carly float, but this gallant effort ended when a searchlight came on and the whole group was wiped out by machine-gun fire.

When the colonel and the eight men of his party landed from the MGB they were, of course, unaware of what had befallen the RSM's party and 'flying timber, smoke, sparks, and flames made it impossible to see very clearly'. Making for his Command Post Newman 'literally bumped into a German' who promptly surrendered. From him the colonel made out that the building he had selected as his HQ was in fact a German one. He sent his prisoner to tell his comrades to surrender, but at this instant a gun opened up at pointblank range, compelling the commandos to take cover. Two vessels from the inner basin and two guns from the roof of the U-boat bunker and a battery on the south bank of the river joined in, and soon the small HQ party was under very heavy fire Troop Sergeant-Major Haines came up with part of Captain Hooper's special task force, whose main task was to destroy two guns between the Old Mole and the Old Entrance. He opened fire with a 2-inch mortar and managed to silence the guns on the U-boat bunker for a time.

One of the demolition parties under Second-Lieutenant H Pennington (Number 4 Commando) never got ashore, but the others lost no time in getting on with their many tasks. Lieutenant Stuart Chant (5 Commando), was hit by shrapnel in the right arm and left leg whilst still aboard the *Campbelltown*. He estimated that something like seventy-five per cent of those on her deck were hit before she rammed the lock gates. He and his men climbed from her bows down scaling ladders and ran like hell to the pumping station. Captain D Roy's assault party had made short work of the gunners on the roof. Chant's men blew the lock off the steel door and went down the steel staircase to lay their charges forty feet below ground. Later Chant described this episode:

'My hands had been cut with small pieces of shell which made the handling of the charge somewhat awkward but Sergeant Dockerill stayed with me in case my wounds should prevent me from firing the charges, while I sent the rest of the party upstairs to warn

Lieutenant Stuart Chant

the neighbourhood of the coming explosion.

'We raced outside and lay on the ground completely exposed on the concrete paving. Fortunately we shifted a further ten yards away a second later, for when the explosion did come huge concrete blocks hurtled through the air perilously near.

'After the explosion we took our remaining explosives in our rucksacks and raced back to the pumping station to complete the work of destruction by blowing up the electric motors and installations'.

They found that the motors had been pitched down below by the collapse of the floor: 'So we just did a little quiet wrecking with sledge hammers and incendiaries'.

Meanwhile Lieutenant Smalley and his party had completely destroyed the winding station near by. These bangs were music in the colonel's ears and he and his HQ party now took up their prearranged position to cover the demolition parties as they fell back across the bridge towards the Old Mole. By this time demolitions were going on all over the place. Newman was joined by his second-in-command, Major Copland, who had landed from the *Campbelltown*. He reported that of one assault party, only the commander, Captain M C Burn, had managed to swim ashore from a stricken ML. He was saved from drowning by Corporal Arthur Young, who grabbed his hair and dragged him along until he reached the Mole. Newman now decided to withdraw Captain Roy's party which was forming a bridgehead on the north side of the connection between the Old Entrance and the Bassin de St Nazaire. Despite the very heavy fire Lance-Corporal Harrington, as cool as if he was on a training exercise at home, got through to Captain Roy with the colonel's message.

Chant, withdrawing his party towards the Old Mole, came to the iron bridge which was covered by a gun in an adjoining building.

'I therefore ordered the men to swing hand by hand, monkey fashion, along the girders under the bridge. Thus we all got across safely unobserved'.

'We gained some railway lines among the warehouses and joined more returning parties. Then came the blow: Colonel Newman told us: "This is where we walk home. All the boats have been blown up or have gone back." '

Newman now had about seventy officers and men with him, but more than half had been hit. The men were behaving magnificently and there was no question of surrender. He held a brief conference with his surviving officers. Some suggested manning some tugs and trying to escape down river.

'Another plan,' wrote Chant, 'was to go down the quayside and swim or wade upstream until we were clear of the German defenders. Colonel Newman, however, decided that the best route was to fight our way back through the warehouses to the east until we reached the bridge.'

The colonel's idea was that the survivors should break up into small groups and make for the Spanish frontier. He ordered them not to surrender until all their ammunition had been used up, and not to surrender at all if they could help it. Their best chance, he said, was to find their way through the town into the open country. 'It's a lovely moonlight night for it.'

Led by Captain Roy and an assault party they moved off and reached the south bank of the Bassin de St Nazaire opposite the U-boat pens. Here Chant was hit in the right knee by a ricochet. His men carried him a little way, but he ordered them to leave him.

'I watched the remainder of the party go south, towards the old part of the town, and then bear right and dash across the swing bridge into the main town. It was bright moonlight, and I could see them clearly. They were fired on from pillboxes and buildings near the bridge; I could see other troops, believed to be Germans, climbing about on the roofs of those buildings.'

The main body, a dwindling band, pushed on, jumping over walls, traversing back gardens, and bursting through houses back to the road.

A German armoured car dashed past 'spitting fire from the turret on all and sundry, including Germans'. Newman's men dodged up an alley. The situation became more and more confused. A German motor-cycle and sidecar was shot up, and the rider and passenger killed.

Eventually Newman, with the twenty or so men who were still with him, took cover in a 'very convenient air raid cellar, complete with mattresses'. Here he intended to stay until next night, when the men would make for the open country in pairs.

'I also decided that if we were found in the cellar I would surrender, as the wounded were in a pretty bad way, and a single hand grenade flung down the stairs would see the lot off.'

Here, some time later, a German party came upon them and accepted Newman's surrender. His men were taken to German headquarters and taken in lorries to a café at La Boule where prisoners were being collected.

Chant, who had been joined by a soldier from another party, was found by three SS men with machine-pistols. 'Heraus! Heraus!' they shouted. 'The soldier with me then stood up with his hands up. He was shot dead from a range of one yard by all three men.' They saw that Chant was wounded and carried him into a café where there were other wounded Commando soldiers.

The brunt of the fighting had fallen on the parties landed from the *Campbelltown* for the MLs had had a very rough time on the run in. Those of the port column were meant to land their troops on the Old Mole. Only one was not destroyed or disabled and only a handful of the men got ashore. Lieutenant I B Henderson, RNVR, unable to bring ML 306 alongside the Old Mole made for the Old Entrance, and, failing to land the Commandos there, turned for home. Some miles downstream he fought an unequal duel with a German MTB. Sergeant Durrant, manning a twin Lewis gun, though riddled with bullets maintained his fire until he collapsed 'sagging over his gun' and died of wounds. With its captain killed and every man aboard dead or wounded the ML was compelled to surrender.

Of the starboard column only the sixth, ML 177, got its party ashore

After the raid, prisoners are rounded up in a bar

The Sten Gun Mk II
The name is derived from the first
letters of the inventors' names
(Sheppard and Tarpin) and the first
letters of Enfield, where the gun was
developed. A cheap and easily produced
weapon, it was made in millions and
was a valued tool of resistance forces
all over Europe. In experienced hands it
was surprisingly accurate and — legend
notwithstanding — perfectly safe for
the user.

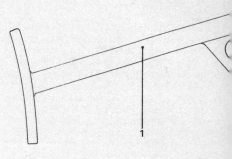

1. Steel tube butt
2. Backsight
3. Block return spring
4. Trigger pin
5. Trigger

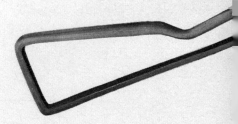

Rate of fire: 500/550 rounds
per minute *Magazine capacity:* 32
rounds, 9mm *Effective range:* 80 yards
Weight: 6.62 lbs *Length:* 30 inches
Muzzle velocity: 1,280 feet per second.

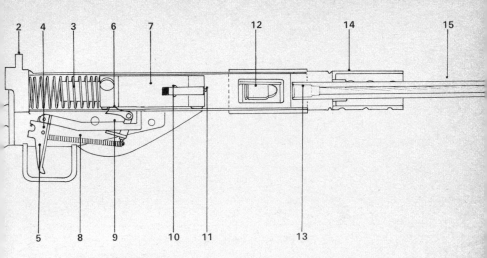

6. Sear	11. Firing pin
7. Breech block assembly	12. 32 9mm rounds
8. Trigger return spring	13. Chamber
9. Trip lever	14. Barrel sleeve
10. Extractor	15. Barrel

HMS Campbelltown wedged in to the sluice gate

more or less intact. TSM Haines landed at the Old Entrance and 'did valiant work all through the operation'. A number of other soldiers managed to swim ashore from abandoned craft, but without weapons.

Three MLs (156, 270 and 446) and the MGB, her decks slippery with blood, reached the rendezvous with *Atherstone* some miles off the estuary of the Loire.

Immediately after the Campbelltown blew up

Meanwhile *Tynedale* had fought an inconclusive action with five German MTBs, and had been hit twice. The crew of ML 156 and the wounded from MGB 314 were transferred to the *Atherstone*, while those from MLs 270 and 446 were put aboard *Tynedale*. The two destroyers, escorted by aircraft of Coastal Command, got back to Falmouth safely. MLs 160, 307 and 443, under Lieutenant T D L Platt, RNR, managed to struggle home on their own. They had hardly a gallon of fuel left. Astonishing though it may seem

they had shot down a German aircraft and damaged another.

When dawn broke after that wild night in St Nazaire there was the old *Campbelltown* 'stuck fast in the lock gates'. Gradually German officers assembled to inspect this phenomenon, while other ranks looked on from the dockside and speculated as to why the British should have carried out such an extraordinary operation. About noon, when there were some forty officers aboard and perhaps 400 German onlookers ashore, the five tons of explosives in the bows of the *Campbelltown* blew up.

There were further explosions at 1630 and 1730 hours when delayed action torpedoes fired through the Old Entrance by MTB 74 went up in the Bassin de St Nazaire. Scenes of considerable confusion ensued, with panicky German soldiers shooting French dock workers, as many as 300 of whom are said to have died, and even members of their own Todt organization. It is said that the panic spread as far inland as Nantes, where

After the raid, an aerial view shows the Campbelltown without her bows 500 yards inside the lock

The aftermath. *Top left:* German troops pass a dead British sergeant *Bottom left:* Soldiers and sailors being led away. *Above:* British pass the bier of a dead comrade

the wives and mistresses of German officers were reported, somewhat improbably, to have run wildly into the streets screaming that the invasion of Europe had begun.

In this raid the Royal Navy lost thirty-one officers and 751 ratings; the Commandos thirty-four officers and 178 other ranks. Five of those left behind managed to make their way back to England via Spain. They were Corporal Wheeler; Lance-Corporals Douglas, Howarth and Sims, and Private Harding. Their success says much for the tenacity and initiative bred by Commando training.

Five Victoria Crosses were awarded for this desperate action. They went to Commander Ryder, Lieutenant-Commander S H Beattie of the *Campbelltown*, to Lieutenant-Colonel Charles Newman, whose resolute spirit had carried his unit to such heights of daring and devotion, and posthumously to Able Seaman Savage and Sergeant Durrant.

The battleship *Tirpitz*, whose potential menace had led to the launching of the raid, remained in the fjords of Norway until in September 1944 12,000 pound bombs from Lancasters of the RAF capsized her near Tromsö.

At the funeral, German officers salute captured British officers

Alarums
and
excursions

'There comes from the sea a hand of steel which plucks the German sentries from their posts.'
Winston S Churchill 1942.

The exponents of the *Blitzkrieg*, so successful in the period 1939-1941, stirred up a bitter resentment which led their victims to fight back by all means in their power. In every occupied country resistance movements grew up, their morale raised by the numerous exploits of British and Allied Commandos, which were faithfully passed on to them by the British Broadcasting Corporation. A time came when no German officer could lie easy in his bed whether in Narvik, Athens or Bayonne. Only at home in the Reich could the dashing Teuton sleep secure, and there his slumbers would be disturbed by the RAF.

As the war went on the landing operations planned by Combined Operations Headquarters became ever larger and more ambitious, Lofoten,

At Athnacarry, Lieutenant-Colonel Charles Vaughan casts a critical eye over Free French Commandos

Vaagso, St Nazaire and Dieppe were all relatively large-scale affairs compared to the raids laid on by Dudley Clarke in 1940. Yet the pin-prick raids carried out by a handful of enterprising and gallant officers and men deserve their place in these pages, if only because they contributed to the general sense of unease which gradually came to pervade the German garrisons of northwest Europe.

But before turning to the smaller raids of 1942 some mention of the Commando system of training seems timely, for it was at this period that an organization tailored for the special requirements of the Commandos came into being.

In December 1942 Achnacarry Castle, the seat of Sir Donald Cameron of Lochiel, the chief of Clan Cameron, became the Commando Depot. For the remainder of the war it was commanded with marked success by Lieutenant-Colonel Charles Vaughan, who had previously been second-in-command of Number 4 Commando. Vaughan had had twenty-eight years service in the Coldstream Guards and the Buffs and knew a very great deal

Training in Scotland. Commandos practice clearing a landing craft

At Inverary, Major Jack Churchill, sword in hand, leads men of 3 Commando ashore from a Eureka

Left and above: Training for the cliff assault. *Below:* In the mountains of Scotland, Commandos learn the techniques of survival

about the ways of the Army. He knew exactly what he wanted and he knew how to get it. His rugged determination to exact the last ounce from his trainees was relieved by a warm heart and a bluff sense of humour, and, though possessed of all the dignity of a former Regimental-Sergeant-Major, he could see a joke against himself. Many were the names in which he rejoiced, ranging from Lord Fort William to The Wolf of Badenoch and The Rommel of the North, but the one which seemed somehow to suit him best was The Laird of Achnacarry. Certainly he loved the place and was fiercely determined that the men who survived his course there and passed out to wear the green beret should do it credit. First and last it is thought that as many as 25,000 men, including US Rangers, Belgians, Dutchmen, Frenchmen, Norwegians and Poles passed through his hands. Vaughan had a hand-picked staff, skilled in devising and running realistic exercises of every kind. Live ammunition was used as a matter of course, and it says much for the skill of the instructors that no more than about forty fatal casualties were suffered during the three years in which the depot was in existence. Feats of activity, such as the celebrated Death Ride in which men crossed the River Arkaig by sliding down a rope, caught the imagination of countless trainees. Men like Alick Cowieson, alias Alick Mor, of the Cameron Highlanders, and CQMS Frickleton, the chief PT instructor, and deviser of the Tarzan Course, displayed a fiendish ingenuity in thinking out such entertainments.

Life at Achnacarry was rugged from the moment the trainees reached Spean Bridge railway station. If they expected transport to take them to the depot they were disappointed: they marched. It is on record that on one occasion an American Ranger, newly arrived, addressed an instructor, Sergeant Taffy Edwards:

'Hey sarge, where's the nearest bar?'
'It's down that way.'
'Yeah? Is it far?'
'No, not far. Only seven miles. It's at Spean Bridge – where your train arrived.'

It does not rain all the time at Achnacarry, but it would be hard to persuade the men who passed through the Commando Depot that that is the case. Far away from the bright lights the men ran up and down mountains by day, became physically fit and acquired confidence and skill at arms. In the evenings, for the good of their souls and in the interests of discipline, they cleaned their brasses, until the day came when their particular intake passed out and Charles Vaughan gave them his closing address:

'When you leave here you will go to civvy billets and get a special allowance. Don't imagine you get this for nothing. You will go on raids and operations.

'Some of you will be wounded. Perhaps badly. Maybe you will lose a leg, or an arm. I tell you now, you don't have to worry. You will be taken care of.' (Dramatic pause) 'There will always be a job for you – up here at Achnacarry.'

To return to the operations, on the night 11th/12th April 1942, Captain Gerald Montanaro RE, accompanied by Trooper Preece, canoed into Boulogne harbour, stuck a limpet (magnetic) mine on a German tanker and withdrew unseen. His canoe was leaky and he was picked up by his parent craft, ML 102, when he was practically waterlogged. Air photographs taken next day showed that the tanker was even more waterlogged – and minus her funnel. Montanaro was awarded the DSO.

The smallest yet one of the best Commando organizations was the Special-Scale Raiding Force, formed by Major Gus March-Phillips, DSO MBE, Captain J G Appleyard, MC, and Graham Hayes, MC. With the welcoming cooperation of its owner, M Stevenson, they formed a base at Anderson Manor, a charming Elizabethan house not far from Poole Harbour, and set out to plague the enemy.

Their first expedition (14th/15th August 1942) was an attempt to destroy an anti-aircraft gun near Cap Barfleur. They launched a Goatley collapsible boat from an MTB, but landing in the wrong place, failed to find their objective. They did, however, kill three Germans.

On the night 2nd/3rd September Appleyard carried out a skilful rai

Captain Gerald Montanaro

on the Casquet Lighthouse, which the Germans, since they took the Channel Islands in 1940, had been using as a naval signalling station. In a letter Appleyard described the midnight adventure:

'I navigated again for the whole job. It was pretty nerve-racking as it's a notoriously evil place and you get a tremendous tide race round the rocks. However, all went well, and we found the place all right, and pushed in our landing craft. My job in the landing and embarkation was 'bow-man'.

'I was the first to leap for the rock, taking a light line with me, and then had to hold the landing craft up to the rock on the bowline whilst Graham [Hayes], in the stern, held the boat off the rock with a stern-line and kedge-anchor he had dropped on the approach, so as to prevent her being dashed on the rock by the swell. There was quite a hefty swell surging up the rocks, and it felt pretty weird in the dark, but we got the whole party ashore safely. The boat was then hauled off the rock on the stern-line by Graham (who remained in her) and I handed over the bowline to the other man who was staying with the boat, and then she rode quite happily until our return.'

They made their way through the barbed wire and gained the courtyard unchallenged. There they dispersed to their pre-arranged objectives. Appleyard and Sergeant Winter dashed up the spiral staircase to the light room,

to find it empty. The garrison was taken completely by surprise. Three were in bed, two were turning in, and two were doing odd jobs. Not a shot was fired, though the Germans had an Oerlikon and two boxes of grenades open. These were dumped in the sea, and then with nineteen men in their landing craft the raiders set off for home. Appleyard was the only casualty. He broke the tibia of a leg whilst re-embarking. They reached Portsmouth to learn that Cherbourg had been 'frantically calling up the Casquets'.

On the night 7th/8th September Major March-Phillips led his men in a raid on St Honoré near the Cherbourg peninsula. Appleyard, because of his damaged shinbone, acted as Navigating Officer. March-Phillips, Hayes and nine others made up the landing party. Finding the objective more heavily guarded than expected, March-Phillips decided to withdraw and return later with a larger force.

On the way back to the beach, and only about 200 yards from the boat, they ambushed and killed a German patrol of seven men. While the major was searching the bodies for maps and documents, another and stronger patrol was heard approaching, and he swiftly got his party back to their craft. When they had paddled one hundred yards from the shore the Germans illuminated them with a flare and opened a heavy fire, which killed March-Phillips and three men, besides wounding several others, and sank the boat. A voice, thought to be

123

Geoffrey Appleyard

Gus March-Phillips

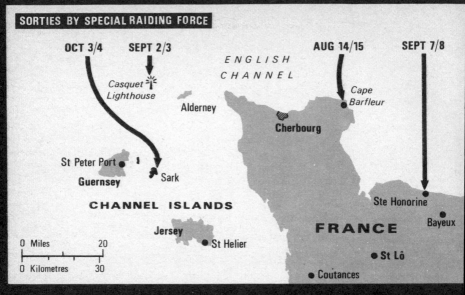

SORTIES BY SPECIAL RAIDING FORCE

OCT 3/4   SEPT 2/3

ENGLISH
CHANNEL

AUG 14/15   SEPT 7/8

Casquet
Lighthouse

Alderney

Cape
Barfleur

Cherbourg

St Peter Port ●
Guernsey   ● Sark

CHANNEL ISLANDS

Ste Honorine

FRANCE   ● Bayeux

0 Miles   20

Jersey
● St Helier

● St Lô

0 Kilometres   30   ● Coutances

The pin-prick raids of 1942. Launched by small groups of commandos, these
raids were designed merely to harass the German forces in the Channel Islands
and on the northern coast of France, with a view to holding German troops in
areas where they would not otherwise be needed, and improving the morale of
the British and French civilian populations.

Graham Hayes's, was heard calling out that all was lost and urging Appleyard to go away and save his ship. The latter did not, however, depart at once. As he searched for survivors his motor boat was hit and one of her main engines put out of action.

Hayes, who had not been hit and was a very strong swimmer, reached the shore some way from the scene of action, got by 'underground' to Paris and eventually to Spain. The Spaniards handed him over to the Germans, and, after nine months in Fresnes prison, he was shot on 13th July 1943.

A Frenchman, André Desgrange, was also taken. He was kept for a time 'shackled so that he could only eat from a trough direct by his mouth'. He escaped to Spain, was imprisoned there, and was treated so badly that although phenomenally strong physically he fainted four times under the treatment. He escaped once again, got back to England, and in three to four weeks returned to France as an agent.

Sergeant-Major Tom Winter had swum, unseen, to within about fifty yards of Appleyard's ship when it received a direct hit and moved out to sea. He managed to reach the beach 'where a German attempted to shoot him as he lay gasping for breath at the water's edge'. The man missed. Winter then saw the Germans beat up another of the party who had just struggled ashore, using their stick grenades as clubs. Later this man's life was saved in a German hospital, but after the war he still suffered serious disablement.

Winter for his part was taken to a prison camp in Poland. He found a way of getting in and out by night, and, contacting the Polish underground instead of endeavouring to escape, instructed them in the use of explosives, returning to camp by dawn each morning! The Germans came to suspect him and he was condemned to ten years solitary confinement. The advance of the Russians set him and thousands more prisoners on the march westwards, and eventually he slipped away and reached the Allied lines.

This disaster was not the end of the SBS. As soon as his leg mended Appleyard began raiding again, and on the night 3rd/4th October visited Sark with a hand-picked party of four officers and five men. They learned much of local conditions and something of the defences from an English woman they met, and captured five Germans in the annexe of the Dixcourt Hotel. These men, though captured in bed, recovered sufficiently to attempt to make their escape and four had to be shot. One of these, a powerfully built man, had his hands tied, which was, technically, an infringement of international law, though since he had refused to 'come quiet' it is difficult to blame his captors for securing him. The upshot of this incident was that Commando prisoners taken earlier, at St Nazaire and Dieppe, were handcuffed as a reprisal.

One of the most effective of all the small raids was Operation Musketoon. Captains Gordon Black and Joe Houghton with a detachment of Number 2 Commando and some Norwegians attacked the hydroelectric power station at Glamfjord in Norway. Landing from a French submarine they approached their objective across a black glacier and attacked it about 2300 hours. There was a brief fight in which one of the guards was killed, and then the machinery and a section of the pipeline were destroyed.

Everything had gone according to plan, and the current that supplied the chief aluminium manufacturing plant in Norway had been destroyed. But few of the raiders made their escape. In a clash with a German patrol Black and Houghton were wounded and captured. Taken to Germany, they were shot in consequence of Hitler's notorious 'Commando Order' of 10th October 1942, laying down that his forces should 'slaughter to the last man all those who take part in Commando engagements'.

This order, unlawful by any rules of warfare, is the measure of the effect which an active raiding policy had had on the precarious balance of Hitler's mind.

Dieppe

'Jesus Christ, sir, this is nearly as bad as Achnacarry.'

Dieppe was the biggest raid carried out by the British during the Second World War. Ten major military units took part, only one of which succeeded in taking its objective. Casualties were heavy, and many people found serious fault with the concept of the whole operation. It is as well to recall that it took place approximately half way between the Dunkirk evacuation, which ended on 4th June 1940, and D-Day, when on 6th June 1944 the Allies invaded Normandy. It was unthinkable that the forces in the United Kingdom should do nothing for four years. The need to show friend and foe alike that Britain was still in the war was in itself sufficient justification for an active raiding policy. Still more important, it was necessary to study the conditions likely to prevail when the Second Front should eventually be launched. There were vital questions to be answered. How strong was Hitler's West Wall? Could the Allies hope to capture a port on D-Day?

There were several reasons for the selection of Dieppe as a target. It was within the range of fighter cover. It was outside any lodgement area likely to be chosen for the D-Day landings. The coast of that part of France has natural defences in its high chalk cliffs, which are similar to those along the English coast between Rottingdean and Newhaven.

The role of capturing Dieppe itself was entrusted to six battalions and an armoured regiment of the 2nd Canadian Infantry Division, which were to land at Puys, Pourville and Dieppe itself. At Berneval and Varengeville were two coast defence batteries, whose guns could bring a crossfire to bear on any ships approaching the beaches. It seemed to the planners that these batteries must be silenced before the main landing. Number 3 Commando was to attack the Berneval Battery and Number 4 that at Varengeville.

Number 4 Commando was commanded by Lieutenant-Colonel the Lord Lovat, MC, whose second-in-command describes him as 'a tall, strikingly handsome fellow who bore

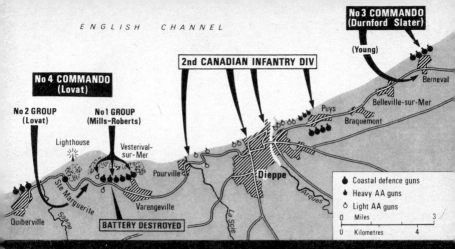

ENGLISH CHANNEL

No3 COMMANDO
(Durnford Slater)

(Young)

Berneval

Belleville-sur-Mer

2nd CANADIAN INFANTRY DIV

No 4 COMMANDO
(Lovat)

Braquemont

Puys

No 2 GROUP
(Lovat)

No1 GROUP
(Mills-Roberts)

Lighthouse

Vesterival-
sur-Mer

Pourville

Dieppe

Ste Marguerite

Varengeville

La Scie

Arques

Saane

Quiberville

BATTERY DESTROYED

Coastal defence guns	●
Heavy AA guns	●
Light AA guns	○

0 _____ 3
Miles

0 _____ 4
Kilometres

he Raid on Dieppe, 18th/19th August 1942. It was planned to land
,000 men with full supporting equipment, but the operation proved to be
nadequately planned and based on false Intelligence. The verdict: 'a costly but

Officers of 1st Commando Brigade watch a demonstration of enemy weapons. Lieutenant-Colonel the Lord Lovat sitting on right. Major Derek Mills-Roberts at microphone

himself well and could take life seriously when necessary'.

The idea of raiding Dieppe was first contemplated in April 1942, so there was ample time for planning and training at unit level. Varengeville is three and a half miles west of Dieppe and the battery lay 1,100 yards inland from the cliffs. There were two possible beaches, one at the mouth of the River Saane near Quiberville and the other directly in front of the battery, where there were two gullies, a fault in the cliff. It was decided to use both beaches. The Commando was, therefore, divided into two main groups. Major D Mills-Roberts commanded Number 1 group, with eighty-eight men to provide covering fire while Lord Lovat commanded 164 men in Number 2 group who were to undertake the assault itself. Lovat's group was the one to land at the mouth of the Saane.

The battery area was reconstructed in outline near Lulworth Cove in Dorset and the Commando rehearsed its full task eight times, until every man could play his part at top speed and carrying his full load of arms

Dieppe at dawn

ammunition, and whatever else it
was his lot to use, be it wireless set,
stretcher or demolition charge. Every
man was thoroughly briefed with the
aid of air photographs and a model
of the objective. Mills-Roberts wrote:
'The Demolition Party could blow
gun breeches in their sleep, communi-
cations had been tested and counter-
tested and the drill for the manning
of the assault craft in the Infantry
Assault Ship *Prince Albert* had been
carried out several times in darkness.
There was the complete list: it was
interesting to speculate what would
go wrong.'

Number 4 Commando had an un-
eventful voyage, was roused at about
0100 hours, breakfasted without enthusiasm, listened to the CO's final
pep talk in the wardroom, and filed
to boat stations.

'D'you think you'll find your crack
in the cliffs all right, Derek?' Lovat
asked his second-in-command.

'Yes, there's no need to worry,' the
latter replied with a conviction he
was far from feeling.

By 0430 hours Mills-Roberts's group
was approaching the beach. Surprisingly enough the lighthouse was
flashing, its beam sweeping across the

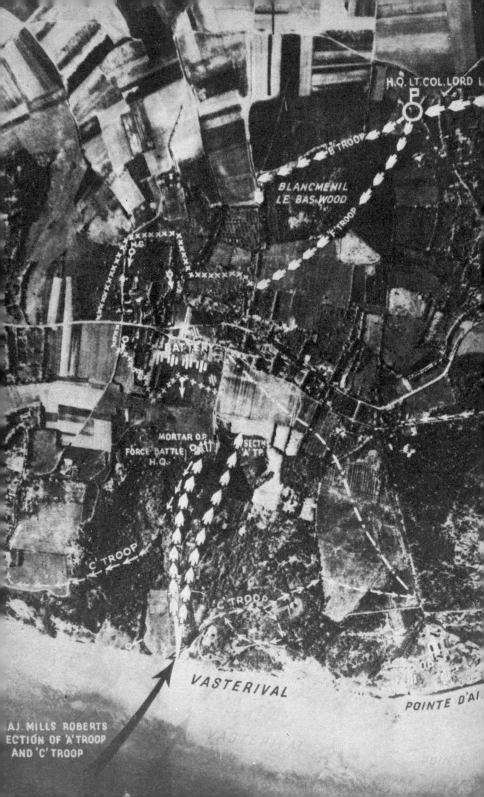

H.Q. LT. COL. LORD L

B TROOP

BLANCMENIL
LE BAS WOOD

F TROOP

M.G.

BATTERY

MORTAR O.P.

FORCE BATTLE
H.Q.

SEC'TN
'A' TP.

'C' TROOP

C TROOP

VASTERIVAL

POINTE D'AI

MAJ. MILLS ROBERTS
ECTIÓN OF 'A' TROOP
AND 'C' TROOP

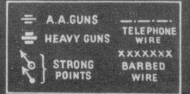

Assault by No 4 Commando on the
six gun battery West of Dieppe

S

E   W

N

MAIN ASSAULT

Ste MARGUERITE

R.S.

EAST END OF CLIFFS

LT.COL. LORD LO
1 SECTN OF 'A' T
'B' TROOP, 'F' TR
H.Q.

A.A.GUNS   TELEPHONE
                  WIRE
HEAVY GUNS
                  XXXXXX
STRONG   BARBED
POINTS   WIRE

landing-craft. 'We felt like thieves in an alley when the policeman's torch shines,' Mills-Roberts wrote later.

The craft were within a mile of the lighthouse when it suddenly doused. Tracer rose into the sky as Brewster Buffaloes roared inland at cliff-top level. It seemed that surprise must have been lost·and the landing craft moved in at their best speed. Close to the cliff they turned to port, cruising along until Lieutenant David Style, sharper eyed than his seniors, spotted the landing place.

Running in the men had a dry landing – it was high tide – and in a matter of seconds were close under the cliff. Style's section reconnoitred the gullies. The left one was choked with thick wire and falls of chalk. A patrol on the flank passed a message: 'There's someone on top of the cliff'. Anxious moments followed as the wire in the right-hand gully was blown with Bangalore torpedoes, but still there was no interference. Fortunately the explosions coincided with heavy firing farther down the coast.

It took some time to reach the top of the promontory between the two gullies, but at length Mills-Roberts and his men were moving towards the villas of the little seaside resort of Vasterival-sur-Mer. He noticed that the gardens looked wild and unkempt. Style's section were searching the houses, and soon produced an old gentleman in a night-shirt, whose garden they had invaded. He seemed very surprised when told that the soldiers were not German but British. The major saw a pretty girl watching from the verandah.

'Are you going to shoot Papa?' she enquired philosophically.

It was now about 0540 hours and, despite delays in the gully, things were going according to plan, for the group still had twenty-five minutes before it had to be in position.

Suddenly, with a tremendous crash, the battery opened fire, and almost immediately the Intelligence Officer, Tony Smith, sent a wireless message from the beach. 'Convoy in sight, apparently within range of enemy battery.' The convoy appeared to be well ahead of schedule. Mills-Roberts decided to dispense with searching the houses between the beach and the

battery and to press on with al speed.

'Corporal Smith and I. Ennis the Mortar Officer and our respective signallers raced up through the wood I had just sent a message to David Style to join us at once. We heard the battery fire six salvoes in close succession. The noise was deafening It was heavy going, as the under growth was waist high. We heard shooting on our right. Any idea o pushing through the undergrowth with stealth was out and we were crashing ahead like a herd of ele phants.

'Suddenly the wood ended. W topped a little rise and came face t face with the battery itself. Ennis an I dropped; so did the others. We worke our way forward to a patch of scrub some fifty yards in front of the woo and about a hundred yards from th perimeter wire of the battery. Ther was a good view from here and w heard the words of command dis tinctly as the battery fired anothe salvo'.

Seeing a barn on the edge of th wood to his right Mills-Robert crawled back to the wood and ra there to find that he now had 'a magn ficent view of the six big guns and th crews serving them' only about 17 yards away. He was just in time t see the three right-hand guns fire salvo. A sniper settled himself on table and took careful aim.

'At last the rifle cracked, it was bull's-eye and one of the Master Rac took a toss into the gun pit. His con rades looked shocked and surprised I could see it all through my glasse. It seemed rather like shooting men bers of a church congregation fro the organ loft'.

The major could not help wonde ing 'how prompt and how effective th German retaliation would be'. Davi Style's section dispersed in the bar area had begun to snipe the gun pi with rifle and Bren gun. The German first reaction was to take cover.

'The gun pits had small parape of sandbags and the crews kept lo within them; and we could now se no movement between the variou battery buildings. Over on the righ there was movement, and the thre right-hand guns fired: no doubt the had been loaded before we had started in and whatever happened they must not be given the chance to load again. We expected trouble, but we did not relish the idea of having those large six-inch guns turned on us. It was up to us to see that they did not load again, either to shell the main convoy or to attempt to destroy the smaller fry to their immediate front'.

The Germans opened up with a 20mm gun from a high flak tower on stilts. The weapon had an all-round traverse. It began to rake the edge of the wood with a stream of phosphorescent shells, which burst against the tree trunks. Fortunately the gunners tended to fire high. A heavy machinegun, probably the one at the northeast corner of the battery, put a wild burst into the wood.

'Suddenly over from some farm buildings on the extreme left of the battery came the phut, phut, phut of German mortars and soon all round us resounded the crash of mortar fire.'

The wood was becoming decidedly unhealthy and Style moved half his section into the scrub, so that they could deal with the eastern end of the battery, as well as being less of a concentrated target.

By this time Mills-Roberts had been joined by two men, Gunner McDonough and Private Davis, with a Boys anti-tank rifle, a long and ponderous weapon, which was already obsolete. But if it would no longer pierce the tanks of the day it proved most effective against the flak tower, which suddenly ceased to revolve.

McDonough could now turn his attentions to the seven heavy machine-guns, sited in the perimeter wire. These had been located beforehand from the air photographs, and were already under accurate fire from the three Bren guns. But the German mortars, as yet unmolested, were still making things uncomfortable, especially in the barn area, where a 2-inch mortar detachment now came into action. Its first bomb fell short; but their next round was a good one and landed in a stack of cordite, behind Number 1 gun, which ignited with a stupendous crash, followed by shouts and yells of pain. We could see the Germans as they rushed forward with buckets and fire extinguishers,

and everything we had was directed on to this area. The fire grew, and meanwhile the big guns remained silent.'

It was 0607 hours.

The Germans were still fighting back. Mills-Roberts had a narrow escape when a mortar bomb landed in a tree above his head, and brought a heavy branch down beside him. Several men had been hit and the medical sergeant, Garthwaite, was mortally wounded, as he went to the assistance of Private Knowles. Another man, Fletcher, 'had all his equipment, and half his clothes blown off by a mortar bomb, while he himself was unhurt'. Style moved his men out of the garden and deployed them further to his left. McDonough and Davis, however, maintained their position in the living quarter of the barn, and when the flak tower opened up again returned its fire with good effect. As the German mortar fire grew still heavier Mills-Roberts's position became ever more precarious. But now, at long last, his 3-inch mortar detachment came into action, and wireless touch was made with Lovat's group. At 0625 hours the battery area was deluged with 2-inch mortar smoke and three minutes later the cannon fighters roared in for their two-minute strike at the guns. On the far side of the battery a Very light soared into the sky. It was the signal for the assault.

Lovat's group, five landing craft (LCAs) and one support craft (LCS), had also increased speed, when at 0430 hours they had seen the white star shells going up from the lighthouse.

Disembarking in the half light they came under fire from mortars and machine-guns as they crossed the heavy beach wire. There were twelve casualties. The Germans were firing tracer, which to men who had not been under fire before seemed most unpleasant. But in fact the casualties were mostly caused by the mortar, which, fortunately, lifted and tried to engage the landing craft as they withdrew.

Three Boston light bombers passed overhead, drawing the enemy fire as the Commandos crossed the wire and dashed across the Quiberville St Mar-

Above: Making smoke to cover the supporting vessels. *Below:* the reception

Above: A Boston over the lodgment area. *Right:* 4 Commando return to Newhaven. Captain Gordon Webb – with arm in sling

guerite road to gain the cover of the east bank of the River Saane. A stream of tracer bullets was whizzing past at about head height. Donald Gilchrist, a subaltern in the leading troop (B) wrote: 'We were forced to run like half-shut knives, our bodies bent forward, as if we were forcing our way against a strong wind.' Lieutenant Veasey scaled the cliff at the east end of the beach, using tubular ladders, and stormed the two pillboxes, sited to defend it. One proved to be unoccupied: the occupants of the other were killed with grenades.

The going was heavy in the long grass for the river had flooded its banks, but by 0515 hours the group had reached the bend where it must break from the cover of the bank and begin its dash eastwards. By this time it was broad daylight. In the distance sustained firing could be heard as Mills-Roberts's group engaged the battery.

The ground between the river and the little wood where the assault force was to form up was not entirely devoid of cover, and open patches were crossed in loose formation by bounds. Reaching the wood B Troop (Webb) and F Troop (Pettiward) divided, according to plan, and began working their way forward towards their forming-up areas.

Through a thick hedge men of B Troop spotted the flak tower. 'Gordon Webb gave the order to fire,' Gilchrist recalls. 'Rifles cracked. We watched amazed as a German soldier toppled over the edge and slowly fell to the ground some eighty feet below – like an Indian from a cliff in a western picture'. Webb sent Gilchrist and a small party to knock out the right hand gun.

'We cut across a hedge, raced through some trees, and darted between two buildings. Before us, not seventy-five yards away, was the battery position, German heads bobbing up and down. We began to stalk – we'd learned how to at Achnacarry – walking upright, stiff-legged, our weapons at the ready. Suddenly we froze.

'A German soldier had appeared from a hedge which ran parallel to and behind the battery. He was carrying a box of grenades.'

Instead of surrendering the man began to shout 'Kommando, Kommando!' like one demented, whereon one of Gilchrist's men, remarking 'I'll give him f— Commando!' shot him. Trooper Marshall got another with his Bren, and someone else landed a hand-grenade in a machine-gun nest. 'Every time a coconut,' said a Cockney voice.

B Troop came under inaccurate fire as it moved round the southern edge of the wood and using the tactics of fire and movement with covering smoke, infiltrated through the orchard to its assembly position, just short of the battery buildings.

At 0625 hours Webb reported by wireless that he was in position for the final assault.

F Troop went through the wood to the point where the track running north leaves it. Thence they advanced under cover of smoke. Reaching a farmyard their scouts came upon a platoon of infantry clustered round the rear of a truck. Firing from the hip, with Bren and Tommy guns, Commandos came round the corner and wiped them out. Thus they disposed of the local 'riot squad' just as it was forming up and drawing grenades and ammunition as a preliminary, no doubt, to a counterattack against Mills-Roberts.

From here on F Troop met with stiff opposition from Germans ensconced in the buildings and enclosures just inside the perimeter of the battery. Pettiward was killed at the head of his men, struck by a stick grenade, and Lieutenant Macdonald was mortally wounded. A sergeant took their place, but was himself killed. Lovat's small HQ group included Captain Pat Porteous, whose role was to ensure liaison between the two assault groups. Porteous now ran across to F Troop, and, taking command, prepared to lead them to the charge. A German attacked him and shot him in the wrist, but Porteous managed to dispose of this assailant with his other hand.

At 0630 hours as the Spitfires of 129 Squadron made off, their brief strike completed, Lovat fired a series of white Very lights, and the assault went in. Webb, whose right wrist had been broken by a mortar bomb on the beach, led his yelling men firing his revolver with his left hand.

'Screams, smoke, the smell of burning cordite. Mad moments soon over'. Thus Gilchrist describes B Troop's part in taking the Varengeville Battery. One ugly episode remained in his mind. He and his men heard a shot and saw a German emerge from a barn and crash his boots into the face of a wounded Commando soldier. A corporal shot the man in the pit of the stomach.

'We doubled across the yard to where the two wounded lay side by side. For our comrade – morphine. For the beast – a bayonet thrust.'

While B Troop cleared the battery buildings Porteous led F Troop with dauntless courage to take the gun sites. Shot through the thigh he was still the first man into the guns, leading the men in a desperate bayonet charge which carried each gun-pit in turn. Troop Sergeant-Major Portman backed him up nobly. Mills-Roberts records that Porteous and Portman 'killed all of one German gun crew and then charged the next gun pit and seized it.'

When a grenade removed the whole of one heel Portman sat on the ground cooly picking off Germans with his rifle. Such was the spirit of the men Lovat led that day. They were not exactly in the mood to be repulsed.

The Germans fought with creditable obstinacy, defending themselves in underground tunnels, the cookhouse and other buildings. Their commanding officer is said to have been bayonetted after an exhilarating chase round the battery office. When the fighting fit ebbed away there were dead Germans everywhere, some badly burnt by cordite. There were only four prisoners, for isolated resistance from mutually supporting pillboxes continued even after the assault had carried the actual gun positions.

The work of demolition began.

Jimmy MacKay (B Troop) told Gilchrist in a satisfied tone that hi

Captain Pat Porteous VC

made-up charges had fitted the guns 'just like a glove'.

The same officer heard Lovat, a debonair figure 'in corduroy slacks and a grey sweater' and armed with a Winchester sporting rifle, give the order 'Set them on fire! Burn the lot,' indicating with a gesture the battery buildings, and comments 'They were the words of a Highland chief bent on the total destruction of the enemy'. It was not only Fraser of Lovat that was motivated by atavistic urges that day. To the British soldier of 1942 Dunkirk was very recent history, and he was tired of hearing about German supermen.

With the Varengeville Battery utterly demolished 4 Commando withdrew in good order, falling back through Robert Dawson's troop, which formed the perimeter round the beach where Mills-Roberts had landed.

It would be hard to conceive of a better planned *coup de main*, or one carried through with more determination. It cost 4 Commando forty-five casualties, including two officers and ten other ranks killed and four missing. Of the twenty wounded, twelve were back at duty within two months. Several of them, like Captain Webb and Lieutenant Style, had carried on after they were hit. The Germans lost not less than 150 killed.

The secrets of this stirring affair were meticulous planning, training and briefing, relentless yet imaginative leadership, and first-class weapon training, the foundation of that self-confidence which is the backbone of courage. In this exploit many won decorations, including the Victoria Cross which was awarded to Captain Pat Porteous.

The task of silencing the Berneval Battery fell to the lot of 3 Commando, the unit which eight months earlier had destroyed the German garrison of Vaagso. Durnford-Slater, who was still in command, decided upon a plan very similar in outline to Lovat's. A strong group under his own command was to land at the beach known as Yellow 1, and a smaller group under the second-in-command, Major Young, was to land at Yellow 2. The plan,

broadly speaking, was to assemble in rear of the battery, near Berneval Church, and to assault the battery in three waves, assault, support and reserve. It was felt that the battery, with perhaps 200 men, would succumb to such an attack by some 450 picked infantrymen. The unit's task was made more difficult because an assault ship was not available and it had to make the whole voyage from Newhaven in 'Eurekas'. These were wooden landing craft, lacking even the thin armour of the LCA. Each craft could carry eighteen fully equipped soldiers.

Number 3 Commando had not been less meticulous in its training than Number 4, but on this occasion Durnford-Slater's usual good fortune deserted him.

At 0347 hours the flotilla ran into a German convoy which was on passage from Boulogne to Dieppe and in the subsequent gun battle was scattered. The SGB in which the colonel had taken passage was hard hit, with forty per cent of its crew and passengers killed or wounded, and in a very short time was out of action. The destroyers which should have escorted the twenty landing craft had gone off up channel for some reason best known to their senior officer, the commander of the Polish warship *Slazak*, and were thus denied the pleasure of an action with five German vessels, which would probably have been easy meat to them.

A number of the Eurekas were more of less severely damaged, whilst others had broken down even before the sea-fight began; they were not designed for a seventy mile channel crossing.

It is not possible for me to discuss this operation in the dispassionate terms of a military commentator since, as it chances, I was second-in-command of Number 3 Commando in this action. I trust I will be forgiven, therefore, if an element of personal reminiscence creeps into the military history at this point!

In the first place I may say that the whole operation seemed 'pretty dicey'. I recall vividly that as we sailed from Newhaven in the dusk I consoled myself with the thought that having survived Dunkirk, Guernsey, Lofoten

Far left: John Durnford-Slater
Left: Peter Young

145

Above: A German medical orderly treats a wounded Canadian. *Below:* A field dressing station. *Right:* 4 Commando disembark at Newhaven

and Vaagso, I had had a fair run for my money.

The sea-fight was a very unpleasant experience. With streams of tracer converging on the wooden landing craft it seemed that death was but an instant away. When the SGB reeled out of action we turned to starboard and made our escape, but in doing so lost contact with all the other landing craft.

Unworthy thoughts assailed me. What good could one do with only eighteen men? However, the officer in charge of our craft, Lieutenant-Commander Buckee, was as skilful as resolute. After a time he said:

'There you are, there's your beach'.

'What do we do now,' I asked, rather pointlessly.

'My orders', he replied, 'are to land even if there's only one boat'.

This aroused the innate obstinacy, or 'bloody-mindedness' which I recognize as one of the less charming facets of my character.

'Those are my orders, too,' I replied. 'We are to land whatever happens, even if we have to swim'.

There are those who contend that the Dieppe raid was not a surprise. To this I can only reply that we could see a lighthouse flashing as we ran in, and that the trenches of the platoon position where we landed were unoccupied. We hit the beach at 0450 hours – five minutes early – and some twenty minutes later had managed to climb the cliff, hauling ourselves up by the barbed wire. The Germans are thorough people and they had put it the whole way up the cliff. The pegs made good footholds. It was daylight when we reached the top and we could see five other landing craft running in to Yellow 1. We could also see the back of a notice board. Walking round to the inland side we read the words ACHTUNG MINEN, but by that time we were through the minefield. I assembled my eighteen followers in a small copse, and gave them the benefit of my views on minor tactics, as well as some rather unconvincing exhortations of the 'Once more unto the breach' variety. Then we set off, moving with a caution that proved unwarranted. The first civilian we met assured

us that there were 200 Germans in the battery.

Before we reached the village the battery opened fire, and throwing caution to the winds we ran down the street to the church, where we hoped to meet the men who had landed from Yellow 1. Instead we came under fire from a German machine-gun, which luckily fired high, bringing a shower of tiles about our ears.

I hoped to snipe the German gunners from the church tower, but the sexton had removed the ladder. Then we tried to work our way up through the orchard behind the battery, but we kept getting fired at by unseen riflemen, and this seemed unpromising. I assembled the party at the western edge of the orchard, where I could see a great cornfield that lay between our landing place and the battery. I decided to deploy the party on the flank of the battery and snipe at the gunners. Some of my followers did not seem altogether persuaded of the beauty of this scheme, but I explained to them that it was well known that nine feet of corn will stop a rifle bullet just as well as, say, eighteen inches of brickwork will.

We doubled out into the field and re-deployed in two lines with big intervals between each man so that the second line could fire through the first. This worked rather well. We had one Bren, but most of the men were armed with rifles. We kept up a steady but not rapid fire, as I wanted to conserve ammunition.

Though we were not 200 yards from the battery our view was not particularly good, as the guns were on the same level as ourselves. We had to fire from the kneeling position, crawling to fresh positions after one or two rounds, and I cannot claim that we caused many casualties for the gunners had low concrete walls to hide behind. Still, if we missed Number 4 Gun, Number 2 would have the benefit of the crack and thump as our bullets winged their way by.

I suppose the gunners fired fifteen or twenty rounds out to sea. I do not think they fired any salvoes. Eventually they got bored with us. Suddenly there was a great explosion, almost in our faces it seemed, though it must have been 150 yards away, an orange

Light naval craft cover the withdrawal

149

flash and a cloud of black smoke. A shell wandered over our heads and landed behind us somewhere in France. The Germans had swung the left hand gun round and were having a go at us. Luckily they could not depress sufficiently to do any harm. Even so it was rather a shattering moment, and the soldier next to me said indignantly: 'Sir! We're being mortared!' Not a very accurate description of the fire of a 6-inch gun.

At Varengeville the Germans had used their mortars to some effect. They do not seem to have had any at Berneval.

They fired their gun at us four times, and we greeted each shot with a volley. Then they gave it up as a bad job. Perhaps they saw that they were not hitting us. Perhaps we knocked out the crew. Weighing the situation impersonally it was, of course, much better that they should fire at us than at the shipping off Dieppe. Looking that way all one could see was a great bank of smoke. From Berneval it was not possible to identify a single target off the town.

Ammunition began to run low and it was clearly only a matter of time until the Germans would produce some force, perhaps supported by tanks, to put in a counterattack.

Highland chief returns from raid

After shooting up the observation post on the cliff, we withdrew. We had had two casualties, but both got away. Buckee had kept his landing craft close into the shore, and we got aboard in the nick of time. Major Blücher and some assault engineers of 181 Division followed us up, and a section reached the cliff in time to fire at us as we departed. In the exchange that followed one of the sailors was hit in the thigh, and a German rifle fell down the cliff.

The craft that landed at Yellow 1 comprised men of several troops. Two of the craft belonged to my old 6 Troop, under Captain Dick Wills, the senior officer present. He led them through a deep bank of wire and thrust inland with vigour. Corporal Banger Halls took a machine gun post, charging single-handed with the bayonet, and a determined effort was made to fan out from the narrow gully. Rhodes, Will's runner, was shot in the fore-arm, had himself patched up, and rejoined his officer with one hand looped round his neck by a bandage and the other grasping an automatic.

The Germans had seen the craft run in, and evidently launched their reserve platoon to hem them in. This left them nothing to spare to counter-attack my party, which, having landed in the dark, was presumably undetected until it reached the church.

Advancing up a narrow road, bordered by villas and hedges, the group made slow progress. Wills, whose eyesight was not remarkable, accounted for one German – probably the best shot of his life – but soon afterwards was shot through the neck. With his fall the momentum went out of the attack, and eventually German reinforcements arrived in considerable force, and the survivors were compelled to surrender.

Despite the ill-fortune that attended Number 3 Commando the Berneval Battery does not appear to have

After Dieppe: the raiding phase closes

scored any hits on the numerous vessels that lay off Dieppe during the raid. It would ill befit me to claim any special significance for this action, but I owe it to the men who were with me that day to say that they played their part with all the *sang froid* which down the years has been the hall-mark of the British soldier at his best.

The Dieppe raid was a costly affair. The Royal Navy had 550 casualties, and lost a destroyer as well as a number of landing craft. Military casualties, mostly Canadian, numbered 3,670 and material lost included twenty-nine Churchill tanks. The Germans admitted a loss of 591 men as well as a number of guns. The Royal Air

Force lost 153 officers and men and 106 planes. The Germans admitted the loss of forty-eight aircraft. Except for 4 Commando's brilliant feat, it cannot be said that the operation was a great success. But it showed the planners that the Allies were not likely to take a port in France on D-Day, whenever that day should dawn. In consequence it was decided to land over the open beaches, towing the Mulberry Harbour, that famous pre-fabricated port, all the way to France. Thus, as so often in war, the right thing happened for the wrong reason.

The soldier's life is full of ups and downs, and the man that cannot take that had better remain a civilian. So I will conclude this sad chapter with a merry tale. It seems that the Germans were very excited at capturing their first Americans, some Rangers who were attached to the Commandos. One, a man of immense height, whose name I wish I could transmit to history, was being interrogated.

German Officer: 'How many American soldiers are there in England?'

US Ranger: 'There are three million. They are all as tall as I am and they have to be kept behind barbed wire to stop them swimming the Channel to get at you bastards.'

Fortunately this particular German had a sense of humour.

Epilogue

'One man is no more than another, if he do no more than what another does.'

The Commando story did not end in 1942, but with the invasion of North Africa on 7th November the whole nature of their role changed. Now began the great series of Allied counter-offensives whose relentless pressure brought the war to an end, with Hitler dead in the ruins of Berlin. In this period of the war, which lasted for approximately two and a half years, the main role of the Commandos was to spearhead large-scale landings by conventional forces, rather than to carry out raids, although sometimes, notably on the east coast of the Adriatic, their mission remained that of those first two years when they had set themselves to torment the *Wehrmacht* between Narvik and Bayonne.

Hard fighting lay ahead for those Commando units that still survived in 1942. Number 1, after a long and hard campaign in North Africa, was to distinguish itself in Burma, during the last campaign on the Arakan coast, especially in the decisive battle of Kangaw. Number 2, rebuilt by Lieutenant-Colonel Jack Churchill after St Nazaire, won further laurels at Salerno and on the shores of the Adriatic. Number 3, after two landings in Sicily and the battle of Termoli, took part in the D-Day landings, went through the whole of the campaign in Normandy, and, later, fought with the Second Army in its advance from the Maas to the Baltic. It may be asserted that no Commando saw more active service than Number 3, though but few of the men that captured Vaagso were still with the unit by the time it crossed the Aller.

Number 4 Commando was another that took part in the long advance from Normandy to the Baltic. At Ouistreham on D-Day, and on Walcheren, it was to display once more the verve and dash of the days when Lord Lovat led it into the Varengeville Battery at Dieppe.

Number 5 Commando, after taking part in the conquest of Madagascar, went to the Arakan, where it played a decisive part in the battle of Kangaw. Number 6 shared with Number 1 the dangers and discomforts of the Tunisian campaign, proving a match for the Hermann Göring Jäger. Later it was with the 1st Commando Brigade in Normandy, Holland and Germany. A unit remarkable for its disciplined courage and its professional skill, it had a moment of sheer, old-fashioned panache, when, with hunting horns sounding and bayonets fixed, it cleared the Aller woods on 8th April, 1945.

Most of Number 9 Commando's active service was in Italy, and the most memorable of its battles was probably the crossing of Lake Commachio.

The various troops of Number 10 (Inter-Allied) Commando, formed under Lieutenant-Colonel Dudley Lister in January 1942, shared the adventures of the British Commandos. The Belgians and Poles, for example, were with Number 2 at Salerno, while the French were with Number 4 in France, and particularly distinguished themselves at the storming of Ouistreham.

Decorations, or the lack of them, are far from being a certain guide to the military virtue of an individual. Many a dogged and skilful soldier has gone through much hard fighting without any special recognition beyond campaign stars, which, after all, are awarded to everyone present who is not discharged with ignominy! Nevertheless the number of awards for gallantry is a useful indication of the effectiveness of a unit or formation. Commando soldiers were awarded eight Victoria Crosses, thirty-seven DSOs and in addition nine bars to that award, 162 Military Crosses with thirteen bars, thirty-two Distinguished Conduct Medals, and 218 Military Medals. In an army where honours and awards were not distributed in lavish fashion, this total of 479 speaks for itself.

Although the Victoria Cross is the only British decoration which can be awarded posthumously a number of the Commando soldiers who won awards did not survive the war. Five officers took part in the raid on Sark. They were Major Geoffrey Appleyard, Captains Colin Ogden-Smith, Dudgeon and Philip Pinkney, and the Dane,

Lieutenant Andy Lassen. Between them they won a VC, a DSO, and six MCs, but unhappily not one of the five lived to see the end of the war. These were exceptionally severe casualties, but other Commandos paid for their triumphs with their persons. When Number 3 Commando went to Normandy in 1944 there were only two officers and a score of men who had been with the unit when it formed. Vaagso, Agnone, and Termoli had taken their toll.

The First Commando Brigade went to Normandy with four units, Numbers 3, 4, 6 and 45 (Royal Marine) Commandos. The Brigadier, Lord Lovat, was badly wounded by a shell during the attack on Breville. Lieutenant-Colonel Robert Dawson (4 Commando) was badly wounded in the assault on Ouistreham, as was the commander of his French troops, Commandant Philippe Kieffer. Derek Mills-Roberts (6 Commando) received a nasty wound in the leg during the defence of Le Plein, but, with his customary resolution, remained to command the Brigade; his second-in-command, Bill Coade, had been hit in the face by a stick grenade on D-Day. On D-Day the commander of Number 3 Commando was twice hit by fragments of shell, while the second-in-command, Major John Pooley, MC, who had been in all the unit's exploits since June 1940, fell in the Merville Battery. The CO of 45 (RM), Charles Ries, was twice wounded on D-Day, and of the brigade's hierarchy only one CO and Major Nicol Grey survived the campaign undamaged.

Not all the Commandos were as unfortunate in this respect as the officers of the Special Boat Section. Of those whose fortunes we have followed in these pages a number went on to play their part in the later phases of the war when the Allies were on the offensive. Charles Haydon and Bob Laycock became major-generals, and the latter was to succeed Lord Mountbatten as Chief of Combined Operations. Lord Lovat, Derek Mills-Roberts, and Peter Young successively commanded the First Commando Brigade, while at the end of the war Ronnie Tod was commanding the Second, and 'ohn Durnford-Slater had

risen to be Deputy Commander of Commando Group. Newman, taken at St Nazaire, was to spend the rest of the war 'in the bag', but was treated with respect by his captors, who even held a parade to celebrate the announcement of the award to him of the Victoria Cross. His successor, the fiery Jack Churchill, after countless adventures, was captured in Yugoslavia. He proved an elusive prisoner and, after several daring attempts, managed to escape during the chaotic final weeks of the war.

A few of the regular soldiers continued in the army after the war, serving in Korea, Jordan and elsewhere. As late as 1969 Brigadier Denis O'Flaherty and Colonel Pat Porteous were still serving. By that date time was beginning to take its toll of the men who a generation earlier had volunteered for special service. There

are many who take pleasure in imagining that 'Britain is finished', and one would have to be complacent indeed to see the England of 1969 as some sort of Utopia. But there was little for comfort in our situation in 1940, and there were plenty of ancient warriors willing to proclaim that the country no longer bred men like the soldiers of the Somme and Passchendaele. No doubt the veterans of Agincourt and Edgehill, of Blenheim and Waterloo, had sung the same song. Nothing is more boring to a young man than to be told that 'things are not what they were'. The Commando soldiers of 1940 may have been rather special in their way – they were all picked volunteers. But they were far from regarding themselves as anything out of the ordinary. Few were of gigantic stature, and, until they had received their specialist

training, few were exceptionally skilful in the martial arts. The great majority had never even been under fire. They were just fed up with being told the Germans were supermen and that they themselves were 'wet'. And so they revolted against their age and went to war in a new spirit of dedicated ferocity. They rejected the lotus years. The politicians of the League of Nations, of Disarmament and of Munich had lost their allegiance, if they ever had it. They revelled in the luxury of responding to uncompromising leadership in a cause that needed no explanation. They approached new tasks in a critical spirit. No tactic was sound just because the book said so. The men who rammed the lock-gates at St Nazaire did a deed every bit as daring as the charge of the Light Brigade at Balaclava, but the old

attitude of 'their's not to reason why' was gone.

A Commando leader once jested bitterly, saying 'An officer is always wrong until he's proved right'. The Commando soldier expected, and rightly, to be clearly briefed; to 'know what he was on'. This was the secret of success in a hundred fights. Intelligent men knew the object of the operation; if things went wrong, if leaders fell, they could use their training, and their native wit, to improvise and to carry on. Battle tactics are no longer the 'Load! Present! Fire!' business of Wellington's day. Happy the commander who has keen, literate, motivated men to carry out his plans! And that is exactly what we had in the Commandos long ago.

Bibliography

Geoffrey J E Appleyard (Blandford Press, London)
Seven Assignments Brigadier Dudley Clarke (Jonathan Cape, London)
The Vaagso Raid Major Joseph H Devins Jr (Robert Hale, London)
Commando Brigadier J F Dunford-Slater (William Kimber, London)
The Watery Maze Bernard Fergusson (Collins, London)
Castle Commando Donald Gilchrist (Oliver and Boyd, London)
Combined Operations 1940–1942 (HMSO, London)
Commando Attack Gordon Holman (Hodder and Stoughton, London)
Geoffrey Keyes of the Rommel Raid Elizabeth Keyes (George Newnes Ltd, London)
Tobruk Commando Gordon Landsborough (Cassell, London)
The Fillbusters John Lodwick (Methuen, London)
The Greatest Raid of All CE Lucas Phillips (Heinemann, London)
Clash by Night Brigadier D Mills-Roberts (William Kimber, London)
The Attack on St Nazaire Commander RED Ryder VC (John Murray, London)
The Green Beret Hilary St. George Saunders (Michael Joseph, London)
Storm from the Sea Brigadier P Young (William Kimber, London)